FocusPrep™

FOCUS	FOUNDATION	PRACTICE

PSAT™ 8/9

3 Practice Tests

for students in grades 8 and 9

Vivek Raghuram

1st EDITION

Published by:

        Gift Of Logic, Inc
        http://www.GiftOfLogic.com

FocusPrep™ is an imprint of Gift Of Logic, Inc.

ISBN-13: 978-1974645015
ISBN-10: 1974645010

8/17, 3/18

Disclaimer:
PSAT 8/9, PSAT 10, PSAT/NMSQT, and SAT are registered trademarks of College Board. College Board does not endorse the materials presented in this workbook. Although every precaution has been taken in the preparation of this book, neither the author nor the publisher shall have any liability to any person or entity with respect to any loss or damage caused or alleged to be caused directly or indirectly by the information contained in this book.

TABLE OF CONTENTS

ORIENTATION & FOCUS   4

PSAT 8/9 Practice Test 1

   Section 1: Reading Test   8
   Section 2: Writing and Language Test   21
   Section 3: Math Test-No Calculator   34
   Section 4: Math Test-Calculator   38
   Answers   45

PSAT 8/9 Practice Test 2

   Section 1: Reading Test   60
   Section 2: Writing and Language Test   72
   Section 3: Math Test-No Calculator   86
   Section 4: Math Test-Calculator   90
   Answers   97

PSAT 8/9 Practice Test 3

   Section 1: Reading Test   113
   Section 2: Writing and Language Test   125
   Section 3: Math Test-No Calculator   137
   Section 4: Math Test-Calculator   141
   Answers   148

Acknowledgments   163

Blank Answer Sheets   167
Scoring Sheets with Answer Key   177
Score Analysis   180

The College Board introduced the PSAT 8/9 in October 2015 for students in grades 8 and 9. You need to **orient** yourself correctly so that you know what content areas are tested, and the details of the format and duration of this test. Once you have oriented yourself, you need to **focus** on the lessons to stay on track and prepare comprehensively. Please read the following questions and answers to learn more about PSAT 8/9.

Q1 How do I **orient** myself to face the PSAT 8/9?

A1 Begin your **orientation** by familiarizing yourself with the SAT suite of assessments shown below. Then, read the questions and answers that follow to get the details of PSAT 8/9. The College Board is introducing PSAT 8/9 for students in grades 8 and 9 to help them track their progress for college readiness. The PSAT 8/9 is aligned with PSAT 10, PSAT/NMSQT, and SAT.

Contact your school counselor for test availability in your school. Visit the College Board website for up to date information. The table below shows the entire suite of PSAT and SAT assessments and the corresponding grades when you take these tests.

Grade	When	Tests	Registration	Purpose
SAT SUITE OF ASSESSMENTS				
NEW PSAT 8/9				
8	Fall or Spring	PSAT 8/9	contact counselor	to track college readiness
9	Fall or Spring	PSAT 8/9	contact counselor	to track college readiness
REDESIGNED PSAT/NMSQT and PSAT 10				
10	Fall	PSAT/NMSQT	contact counselor	check college readiness
10	Spring	PSAT 10	contact counselor	check college readiness
11	Fall	PSAT/NMSQT	contact counselor	check college readiness; National Merit Qualifier
REDESIGNED SAT				
11	Spring	SAT	register online	college admission
12	Fall	SAT	register online	college Admission

Q2 What subjects are tested and how many questions are there in PSAT 8/9?

A2 The breakup of the PSAT 8/9 test is shown below.

Section	Questions, Duration, and Content
Reading Test	5 passages-55 minutes -42 questions Topic tested include: Argumentation, Command of evidence, Words in context, Information and ideas, Infographics. • One passage from a classic or contemporary work of US or World literature • One passage or a pair of passages from either a U.S founding document (declaration of independence, bill of rights) or a text in the great global conversation (speeches by Edmund Burket, Nelson Mandela, Mohandas Gandhi, etc) regarding human dignity, freedom and justice. • One passage about economics, psychology, sociology, or some other social science topic • Two science passages (or one passage and one paired passage) that examine foundational concepts and developments in Earth Science, Biology, Chemistry or Physics.
Writing and Language	4 passages-30 minutes-40 questions Topic tested include: Sentence structure, precision, syntax, style, and tone, improving word choice, sentence and paragraph sequencing, choosing relevant ideas, editing the main idea, and Infographics. • Passages about careers – e.g Working as a computer engineer, or a transportation planner • Passages on Humanities- From U.S. history or the Great Global Conversation • Passages about Science- short academic papers
Reading and Writing Score: Minimum: 120 Maximum: 720	
Math- No Calculator	20 minutes- 13 questions (10 Multiple Choice + 3 Grid In) (8 Heart Of Algebra + 5 Passport to Advanced Math)
Math- Calculator	40 minutes-25 questions (21 Multiple Choice + 4 Grid In) (16 Problem Solving and Data Analysis + 8 Heart of Algebra + 1 Passport to Advanced Math)
	Topics tested in Math sections include: Numbers and Operations, Factors and Multiples, Word problems, Ratio, Rate, and Variation, Percentages, Unit Conversions, Scatterplots, Graphs and Tables, Growth and Decay, Statistics, Population and Sample, Counting, Probability, Linear Equations, System of Linear Equations, Linear Inequalities, System of Linear Inequalities, Linear Models and Graphs, Absolute Equalities and Inequalities, Polynomials and Quadratics , Linear- Quadratic Systems, Functions and Transformations, Radicals and Fractional Exponents

Math Score: Minimum: 120 Maximum: 720	
Total PSAT 8/9 Score: Minimum: 240 Maximum: 1440	145 minutes 42 Evidence-based Reading questions + 40 Writing & Language questions 25 Math Calculator questions + 13 Math No-Calculator questions

Q3 How do I **focus** and prepare with a strong **foundation** for the PSAT 8/9 Test?

A3 Two separate workbooks are available from Amazon.com to help you prepare for the test.

- PSAT 8/9 Reading and Writing Workbook
- PSAT 8/9 Math Workbook.

The following table shows the table of contents of these two workbooks. We strongly recommended you to get familiar with the lessons in the workbooks before you take the three practice tests in this book.

PSAT 8/9 Workbooks	Lessons
PSAT 8/9 Reading and Writing Workbook ISBN 978-1541377974 Search for "PSAT 8/9" in Amazon.com	Lesson 1-Argument passage Lesson 2-Command of evidence questions Lesson 3-Words in context questions Lesson 4-Information and ideas passage Lesson 5-Infographics passage Lesson 6-Paired passages Lesson 7-Verb tenses Lesson 8-Sentence structure conventions Lesson 9-Precision, syntax, style, and tone Lesson 10-Improving word choice Lesson 11-Sentence sequencing Lesson 12-Paragraph sequencing Lesson 13-Choosing relevant ideas Lesson 14-Main idea Lesson 15-Infographics
PSAT 8/9 Math Workbook ISBN 978-1512373776 Search for "PSAT 8/9" in Amazon.com	Lesson 1-Numbers and Operations Lesson 2-Factors and Multiples Lesson 3- Word problems Lesson 4-Ratio, Rate, and Variation Lesson 5-Percentages Lesson 6-Unit Conversions Lesson 7-Scatterplots Lesson 8-Graphs and Tables Lesson 9-Growth and Decay Lesson 10-Statistics

	Lesson 11-Population and Sample
	Lesson 12-Counting
	Lesson 13-Probability
	Lesson 14-Linear Equations
	Lesson 15-System of Linear Equations
	Lesson 16-Linear Inequalities
	Lesson 17-System of Linear Inequalities
	Lesson 18-Linear Models and Graphs
	Lesson 19-Absolute Equalities and Inequalities
	Lesson 20-Polynomials and Quadratics
	Lesson 21-Linear- Quadratic Systems
	Lesson 22-Functions and Transformations
	Lesson 23-Radicals and Fractional Exponents

Q4 How do I use this book?

A4 We recommend the following 3-week plan to prepare for PSAT 8/9.

Week	Task
1	Cut out the answer sheets for practice test 1 from the end of this book. Take practice test 1. Follow the time limit indicated on top of each section. Score your answers. Get your raw score. Identify the areas needing improvement. Review the PSAT 8/9 Reading/Writing and Math Workbooks (available in Amazon).
2	Cut out the answer sheets for practice test 2 from the end of this book. Take practice test 2. Follow the time limit indicated on top of each section. Score your answers. Get your raw score. Identify the areas needing improvement. Review the PSAT 8/9 Reading/Writing and Math Workbooks (available in Amazon).
3	Cut out the answer sheets for practice test 3 from the end of this book. Take practice test 3. Follow the time limit indicated on top of each section. Score your answers. Get your raw score. Identify the areas needing improvement. Review the PSAT 8/9 Reading/Writing and Math Workbooks (available in Amazon).

Questions 1-8 are based on the following passage.

Passage 1

Read the following excerpt from *The Secret Garden* by Frances Burnett and answer the questions that follow.

(1)　　　When Mary Lennox was sent to Misselthwaite Manor to live with her uncle everybody said she was the most disagreeable-looking child ever seen. It was true, too. She
(5) had a little thin face and a little thin body, thin light hair, and a sour expression. Her hair was yellow, and her face was yellow because she had been born in India and had always been ill in one way or another. Her father had held a
(10) position under the English Government and had always been busy and ill himself, and her mother had been a great beauty who cared only to go to parties and amuse herself with happy people. She had not wanted a little girl at
(15) all, and when Mary was born she handed her over to the care of an Ayah, who was made to understand that if she wished to please the Mem Sahib she must keep the child out of sight as much as possible.
(20)　　　So when she was a sickly, fretful, ugly little baby she was kept out of the way, and when she became a sickly, fretful, toddling thing she was kept out of the way also. She never remembered seeing familiarly anything
(25) but the dark faces of her Ayah and the other native servants, and as they always obeyed her and gave her her own way in everything, because the Mem Sahib would be angry if she was disturbed by her crying, by the time she
(30) was six years old she was as tyrannical and selfish a little pig as ever lived. The young English governess who came to teach her to read and write disliked her so much that she gave up her place in three months, and when

(35) other governesses came to try to fill it they always went away in a shorter time than the first one. So if Mary had not chosen to really want to know how to read books she would never have learned her letters at all.
(40)　　　One frightfully hot morning, when she was about nine years old, she awakened feeling very cross, and she became crosser still when she saw that the servant who stood by her bedside was not her Ayah.
(45)　　　"Why did you come?" she said to the strange woman. "I will not let you stay. Send my Ayah to me."
　　　The woman looked frightened, but she only stammered that the Ayah could not come
(50) and when Mary threw herself into a passion and beat and kicked her, she looked only more frightened and repeated that it was not possible for the Ayah to come to Missie Sahib.
　　　There was something mysterious in the
(55) air that morning. Nothing was done in its regular order and several of the native servants seemed missing, while those whom Mary saw slunk or hurried about with ashy and scared faces. But no one would tell her anything and
(60) her Ayah did not come. She was actually left alone as the morning went on, and at last she wandered out into the garden and began to play by herself under a tree near the veranda. She pretended that she was making a flower-
(65) bed, and she stuck big scarlet hibiscus blossoms into little heaps of earth, all the time growing more and more angry and muttering to herself the things she would say and the names she would call Saidie when she returned.

1. The word "sour" in line 6 most nearly means:

A) Sweet
B) Bitter-tasting
C) Acidic
D) Resentful

2. Which of the following lines best describes why Mary's face was yellow?

A) Line 1-4 ("When Mary... ever seen")
B) Lines 4-6 ("She had...expression")
C) Line 8-9 ("born...another")
D) Lines 9-11 ("Her father...himself")

3. It can be inferred through the passage that Mary's mom:

A) Enjoyed taking care of Mary
B) Did not care for Mary's upbringing
C) Relied on Mary's father to raise her
D) Wished for Mary to be given to adoption

4. Which choice most effectively supports the answer to the previous question?

A) Lines 4-6 ("She had...expression")
B) Line 12-14 ("great...people")
C) Lines 14-19 ("She had...possible")
D) Line 20-23 ("So when...also")

5. Lines 29-31 ("by the time... ever lived") use which of the following rhetorical techniques?

A) Simile
B) Idiom
C) Onomatopoeia
D) Allusion

6. The word "governess" in line 32 most nearly means:

A) Servant
B) Teacher
C) Maid
D) Merchant

7. Lines 48-53 best describe Mary as:

A) Spoiled
B) Intelligent
C) Mesmerizing
D) Adventurous

8. The final paragraph of the excerpt causes the reader to feel:

A) Argumentative
B) Sad
C) Excited
D) Suspenseful

Questions 9-17 are based on the following passage.

Passage 2

Read the following excerpt on the causes of the American Civil War and answer the questions that follow.

(1)　　　The Civil War is the central event in America's historical consciousness. While the Revolution of 1776-1783 created the United States, the Civil War of 1861-1865 determined
(5)　what kind of nation it would be. The war resolved two fundamental questions left unresolved by the revolution: whether the United States was to be a dissolvable confederation of sovereign states or an
(10)　indivisible nation with a sovereign national government; and whether this nation, born of a declaration that all men were created with an equal right to liberty, would continue to exist as the largest slaveholding country in the world.
(15)　　　Northern victory in the war preserved the United States as one nation and ended the institution of slavery that had divided the country from its beginning. But these achievements came at the cost of 625,000 lives-
(20)　-nearly as many American soldiers as died in all the other wars in which this country has fought combined. The American Civil War was the largest and most destructive conflict in the Western world between the end of the
(25)　Napoleonic Wars in 1815 and the onset of World War I in 1914.
　　　The Civil War started because of uncompromising differences between the free and slave states over the power of the national
(30)　government to prohibit slavery in the territories that had not yet become states. When Abraham Lincoln won election in 1860 as the first Republican president on a platform pledging to keep slavery out of the territories, seven slave
(35)　states in the deep South seceded and formed a new nation, the Confederate States of America. The incoming Lincoln administration and most of the Northern people refused to recognize the legitimacy of secession. They feared that it

(40)　would discredit democracy and create a fatal precedent that would eventually fragment the no-longer United States into several small, squabbling countries.
　　　The event that triggered war came at
(45)　Fort Sumter in Charleston Bay on April 12, 1861. Claiming this United States fort as their own, the Confederate army on that day opened fire on the federal garrison and forced it to lower the American flag in surrender. Lincoln called
(50)　out the militia to suppress this "insurrection." Four more slave states seceded and joined the Confederacy. By the end of 1861 nearly a million armed men confronted each other along a line stretching 1200 miles from Virginia to
(55)　Missouri. Several battles had already taken place--near Manassas Junction in Virginia, in the mountains of western Virginia where Union victories paved the way for creation of the new state of West Virginia, at Wilson's Creek in
(60)　Missouri, at Cape Hatteras in North Carolina, and at Port Royal in South Carolina where the Union navy established a base for a blockade to shut off the Confederacy's access to the outside world.
(65)　　　But the real fighting began in 1862. Huge battles like Shiloh in Tennessee, Gaines' Mill, Second Manassas, and Fredericksburg in Virginia, and Antietam in Maryland foreshadowed even bigger campaigns and
(70)　battles in subsequent years, from Gettysburg in Pennsylvania to Vicksburg on the Mississippi to Chickamauga and Atlanta in Georgia. By 1864 the original Northern goal of a limited war to restore the Union had given way to a new
(75)　strategy of "total war" to destroy the Old South and its basic institution of slavery and to give the restored Union a "new birth of freedom," as President Lincoln put it in his address at Gettysburg to dedicate a cemetery for Union
(80)　soldiers killed in the battle there.

9. Lines 11-14 ("and whether...world") imply that:

A) The United States did not grant equal liberties to everyone before the Civil War
B) Slaves in the United States were illegal before the Civil War
C) The United States could not be divided over an issue like slavery
D) The Civil War is an important event in American history

10. Which of the following is best supported by the passage?

A) The constitution of the United States was created after the Civil War
B) Slavery should continue to be legal in the future
C) The outcome of the Civil War was a positive one
D) World War 1 was a larger battle than the Civil War

11. Which choice most effectively supports the answer to the previous question?

A) Lines 1-2 ("The...consciousness")
B) Lines 13-14 ("would...country")
C) Line 15-19 ("Northern...cost")
D) Line 20-22 ("nearly...combined")

12. The word "uncompromising" in line 28 most nearly means:

A) Flexible
B) Interesting
C) Composting
D) Inflexible

13. The author makes which of the following claims about President Abraham Lincoln?

A) Lincoln was completely against the idea of slavery in the United States
B) Lincoln believed that secession would lead to the fragmentation of the US
C) Lincoln supported the creation of several smaller countries
D) Lincoln followed his administration even though he did not believe in their ideas

14. The word "triggered" in line 44 most nearly means:

A) Cannoned
B) Shot
C) Started
D) Annoyed

15. Paragraph 4 of this passage provides the reader with:

A) A catalog of the war tactics used by the Union soldiers to defeat the Confederacy
B) A list of the literary works published in relation to the events of the Civil war
C) The reasons for the end of the Civil War
D) A summary of the beginning of the Civil War

16. The author's point of view is:

A) First person
B) Second person
C) Third person omniscient
D) Third person limited

17. The main idea of this passage is that

A) The Civil War had a lasting impact on American history due to the violent nature of the conflict
B) The outcome of the Civil War could have been different if the Union had surrendered
C) The Civil War was an unnecessary battle that had no historical importance
D) Fort Sumter was the most important battle of the entire Civil War

Questions 18-25 are based on the passage below.

Passage 3

Read the following excerpt from History.com discussing the formation of black holes and answer the questions that follow.

(1) According to data picked up by the Laser Interferometer Gravitational-Wave Observatory (LIGO), the two black holes that smashed together some 3 billion light-years from here were large in themselves, measuring
(5) 19 and 32 times the mass of the sun. But when they merged, they created a monster.

Such a dramatic merger may seem alarming, but it appears we should start getting used to it. This is the third black-hole collision
(10) scientists have reported in less than two years, suggesting such events might occur quite frequently in the distant reaches of space.

During a news conference yesterday announcing the detection of gravitational waves
(15) from the latest collision (which occurred back on January 4), LIGO's team of scientists said collisions between massive black holes are so common that they expect to start detecting as many as one per day once the observatory
(20) begins operating at its full capacity.

LIGO's observations come from two detectors—located in Hanford, Washington, and Livingston, Louisiana—and are analyzed by an international collaboration of more than
(25) 1,000 scientists. Though the observatory began operating in 2002, it wasn't sensitive enough to detect much of anything until it underwent a major upgrade, known as Advanced LIGO, which was completed in late 2014.

(30) In September 2015, during a test run several days before the official search began, Advanced LIGO detected gravitational waves for the first time in history. These ripples in the fabric of space and time, caused by a black-hole
(35) collision some 1.3 billion light years from Earth, provided the first concrete evidence of a phenomenon first proposed by Albert Einstein in 1916 in his theory of general relativity.

By the time scientists announced that
(40) mind-blowing discovery in February 2016, LIGO had already picked up waves from a second black-hole collision in late 2015—on Christmas Day, no less. The third black-hole merger, announced this week, occurred much further
(45) away than the previous two. The gravitational waves it caused had to travel some 3 billion light-years to get here, compared with 1.3 billion and 1.4 billion light-years, respectively, for the first two. In addition, the latest merger
(50) revealed some new, intriguing clues about how the two black holes were moving in relation to each other, and even how they may have formed in the first place.

Pairs of black holes not only spiral
(55) around each other, but they also spin individually on their own axes, just like the Earth and most other planets do. A statement from LIGO about the new discovery, Whitney Clavin of the California Institute of Technology
(60) (Caltech) describes this dynamic "like a pair of ice skaters spinning individually while also circling around each other."

When black holes in a pair spin in the same orbital direction as the pair is moving,
(65) they're what's called "aligned." But LIGO's observations of the two black holes that collided in the latest merger suggest that at least one of them was "non-aligned," meaning it was spinning in the opposite direction from
(70) the pair's orbital motion.

This non-alignment is important because scientists have proposed two theories about how binary pairs of black holes can form: first, they could come into being at the same
(75) time, when a pair of stars explodes; second, they could form separately and pair up later in life, in the middle of a dense cluster of stars. In the first scenario, the black holes would likely remain aligned, while in the second they could
(80) spin in any direction in relation to their orbital motion.

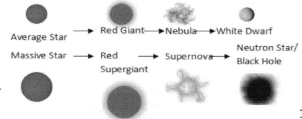

18. The word "merged" in line 6 most nearly means:

A) Combined
B) Exploded
C) Caved
D) Folded

19. Which of the following statements is supported by the passage?

A) Black holes have been discovered recently and are perplexing phenomenon
B) It is difficult to analyze black holes since they are so far away from the Earth
C) The collision of the two large black holes may be frightening to the public
D) Black holes near the earth continue to merge on an hourly basis

20. Which choice most effectively supports the answer to the previous question?

A) Lines 1-4 ("According...here")
B) Lines 4-5 ("measuring...sun")
C) Lines 7-9 ("Such...to it")
D) Lines 9-12 ("This...space")

21. Which of the following is a way by which scientists have analyzed data collected from black holes?

A) Using a telescope along with Hanford's laws of gravitation to determine the position shift of black holes
B) Analyzing data collected from a combination of black hole detectors throughout the world
C) Comparing the annual black hole shift between the years 2002 and 2014
D) Relying on equations provided by Newton and Galileo to determine parallax shifts in space

22. The word "ripples" in line 33 most nearly means:

A) Waves
B) Droplets
C) Tears
D) Mixers

23. According to the passage, which of the following is not true about a pair of black holes?

A) A pair of black holes spiral around each other
B) A pair of black holes can combine to create a more massive black hole
C) A pair of black holes spin on their own separate axes
D) A pair of black holes can exert equal gravitational forces, causing them to disintegrate

24. The main idea of this passage is that

A) Scientists are in the process of discovering more information about binary pairs of black holes
B) Black holes cannot be studied as they naturally exist in pairs
C) The comparison of binary stars has led to new discoveries in the composition of binary black holes
D) Scientists have discovered new processes in the formation of a blue main sequence star

25. The sun is not considered to be a massive star. According to the diagram in the passage, which of the following bodies could be the final stage of the sun's life cycle?

A) Neutron Star
B) Black Hole
C) White Dwarf
D) Supernova

Questions 26-34 are based on the excerpts below.

Passage 4

Excerpt 1

The following excerpt is from a speech made by the German philosopher Moses Hess, who supported socialism, in February 1845.

(1)   Gentlemen, there is no point in talking to you about the intellectual, moral and physical misery of today's society. Any man with a heart, however favorable his position, will
(5) agree with me, when he looks at this world of misery, that our life is not happy. I just want to draw to your attention that the basic cause of all the ills of present-day society, which is normally attributed to the imperfection of
(10) human nature, is in fact the lack of organization of human society. I have already also often heard it said that the idea of communism, fine and true in itself, is unfortunately unrealizable. If I am not mistaken, it is these two points,
(15) concerning the possibility of realizing communism and the fundamental cause of human miseries, which most need to be spelt out. In order to make the best use of the short time which has been given us to deal with our
(20) subject, I think I will limit myself to elucidating a little further these two themes.
       The idea of communism, gentlemen, with which everyone says he agrees, is the life-law of love applied to social life. The law of love
(25) is innate in man, as in all life, but attempts to apply this law to social life will only be made when men's consciousness of their life has begun to mature in them, when they come to see more and more clearly their own existence,
(30) when they understand more and more clearly that it is precisely and solely in love that energy, the energy of life, creative energy lies.

Excerpt 2

The following excerpt is from Senator Joseph McCarthy's speech in February 1950, accusing many members of the US government of going against the United States and supporting communism.

(33)   Six years ago, there was within the Soviet orbit, 180,000,000 people. Lined up on
(35) the anti-totalitarian side there were in the world at that time, roughly 1,625,000,000 people. Today, only six years later, there are 800,000,000 people under the absolute domination of Soviet Russia—an increase of
(40) over 400 percent. On our side, the figure has shrunk to around 500,000,000. In other words, in less than six years, the odds have changed from 9 to 1 in our favor to 8 to 5 against us.

     This indicates the swiftness of the
(45) tempo of Communist victories and American defeats in the cold war. As one of our outstanding historical figures once said, "When a great democracy is destroyed, it will not be from enemies from outside, but rather because
(50) of enemies from within."

     The reason why we find ourselves in a position of impotency is not because our only powerful potential enemy has sent men to invade our shores, but rather because of the
(55) traitorous actions of those who have been treated so well by this Nation. It has not been the less fortunate, or members of minority groups who have been traitorous to this Nation, but rather those who have had all the benefits
(60) that the wealthiest Nation on earth has had to offer: the finest homes, the finest college education, and the finest jobs in government we can give.

     This is glaringly true in the State
(65) Department. There the bright young men who are born with silver spoons in their mouths are the ones who have been most traitorous.

     I have here in my hand a list of 205, a list of names that were made known to the
(70) Secretary of State as being members of the Communist Party and who nevertheless are still working and shaping policy in the State Department.

     As you know, very recently the
(75) Secretary of State proclaimed his loyalty to a man guilty of what has always been considered as the most abominable of all crimes—being a traitor to the people who gave him a position of great trust—high treason.

(80)   He has lighted the spark which is resulting in a moral uprising and will end only when the whole sorry mess of twisted, warped thinkers are swept from the national scene so that we may have a new birth of honesty and
(85) decency in government.

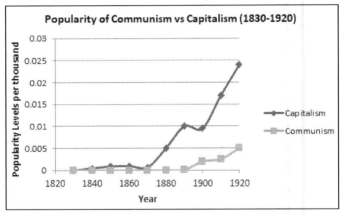

26. The speaker's attitude in lines 1-6 can be described as:

A) Depressed
B) Persuasive
C) Detached
D) Melancholic

27. The word "ills" in line 8 most nearly means:

A) Disenfranchisements
B) Medications
C) Sickness
D) Problems

28. The main idea of excerpt 1 is that:

A) the idea of communism should not be propagated further in society
B) communism is a viable solution to save human society
C) there is no point in talking about communism as it is not a useful idea
D) the previously created utopian societies showcase the success of communism

29. Lines 33-43 support the author's argument that:

A) the shrinking figures of the American population has allowed communism to thrive
B) the Russians do not have enough people to sustain a communistic regime
C) communism remains a better form of society than capitalism
D) the communistic forces of the Soviets have begun taking over the world

30. The word "tempo" in line 45 most nearly means:

A) Conditioning
B) Rate
C) Time
D) Expedition

31. The author uses lines 46-50 ("As...within") to:

A) accuse members of the US government of being communist spies
B) provide a solution for the destruction of the US government
C) use a quote by a historical figure to persuade the audience to believe him
D) remove all communists from the US government immediately

32. The graph shown in the passage detailing the growth of communism and capitalism best supports the argument of which author?

A) McCarthy
B) Hess
C) Both McCarthy and Hess
D) Neither McCarthy nor Hess

33. All of the following statements are true EXCEPT:

A) The author of excerpt 1 would not support the argument of excerpt 2
B) The author of excerpt 2 would not support the argument of excerpt 1
C) The author of excerpt 1 would support the argument of excerpt 2
D) The argument of excerpt 1 contradicts the argument of excerpt 2

34. Which author would support the idea that communism does not generate a perfect society?

A) McCarthy
B) Hess
C) Both McCarthy and Hess
D) Neither McCarthy nor Hess

Questions 35-42 are based on the passage below.

Passage 5

Read the following article on Cormorants from Popular Science and answer the questions that follow.

(1)   Cormorants, with their distinct silhouette and dark feathers, are master fishermen who dive deep into the sea in pursuit of prey. Of the 40 species of cormorant in the
(5) world, all are gifted swimmers, but only one— located in the remote Galapagos Islands—has lost the ability to fly.

In a paper published on Thursday in Science, biologists and geneticists figured out
(10) how the bird got grounded.

Flightless birds have been a source of fascination for evolutionary scientists since the days of Darwin. Ostriches, emus, kiwis, and penguins have all had their lack of flight ability
(15) explored, from their feathers to muscles to bones. But with the Galapagos cormorant, geneticists had a unique opportunity to zero in on the genetic roots of flightlessness.

The Galapagos cormorant last shared a
(20) common ancestor with flighted cormorants two million years ago, which is an incredibly short time in evolutionary terms. For comparison, humans and chimpanzees last shared a common ancestor roughly seven million years
(25) ago if not even earlier. Ostriches and kiwis shared common ancestors with flighted relatives millions of years before that. The relatively short evolutionary distance between Galapagos cormorants and other (flighted)
(30) species makes these birds ideal candidates for looking at genetic changes that might underpin the physical differences that separate the species.

In the new paper, the researchers
(35) noted that when they compared the genome of the flightless cormorant to three flighted species, there was a distinct mutation found around genes that regulated the formation of cilia, or tiny structures that form on cells from

(40) green algae to humans. Cilia have different functions in different organisms, but in vertebrates like cormorants and people, one of their functions is regulating skeletal development.

(45)   "One way to think about flightless cormorants is to think of overgrown big chicks," says lead study author Alejandro Burga. Many features of the Galapagos cormorant, including a short keel (an extension of the breastbone)
(50) and small wings, resemble the juvenile stage of cormorants. Mutations on genes related to cilia or skeletal growth could help change the birds' skeletal structure in this way.

They tested whether or not these genes
(55) would significantly alter cilia by altering genes in the same way in mouse cells and C. elegans, a nematode frequently used in biological research. While cilia in these tiny worms serve a very different function than they do in
(60) vertebrates, the researchers found that the cilia in the nematodes and the mouse cells were significantly altered.

So why would this mutation have persisted in the Galapagos population? It could
(65) be that with an abundance of food and a lack of predators, they simply lost the need to fly. Being flightless may also have helped the birds redirect their energy resources towards size, or let them become better swimmers, like
(70) penguins, able to dive deep and access fishing areas off-limits to competitors.

"The Galapagos cormorant is the largest cormorant despite having the smallest wings," Burga says. "Maybe it is beneficial."
(75)   But, he adds, there is no reason that it couldn't be some combination of those factors. They might have both lost the need to fly and gained advantages from not flying at the same time. Neither explanation is mutually exclusive.
(80)   Burga and his colleagues still have a lot of questions that they want to answer. "There is still a lot to know and understand," Burga says. "Is it something that is unique or is it something that has evolved in different birds? Can we find
(85) the same genes that have been affected in other birds? Are the mutations responsible for

morphological changes in other animals, including primates?"

The last question is especially
(90) interesting for humans. Humans can develop sometimes lethal skeletal ciliopathies or diseases related to cilia development that affect the bones. It's not a one-to-one comparison, but understanding more about how these genes
(95) function in other animals could lead to a greater understanding of how they might manifest in our own species.

35. Which of the following characteristics of the Galapagos Cormorant has caused scientists to research its genetic background?

A) Its ability to swim efficiently
B) Its ability to pursue fast-moving prey
C) Its ability to blend into the dark waters using its specially colored feathers
D) Its inability to fly

36. What is the significance of the phrase "evolutionary distance" as it is used in this passage?

A) The difference between ostriches and cormorants in terms of evolution
B) A reference to the fact that the Galapagos cormorant cannot fly
C) The distance that a human can walk in comparison to a chimpanzee
D) A reference to the years between evolutionary changes in a certain species

37. The word "genome" in line 35 most nearly means:

A) Genes
B) Gnomes
C) Organism
D) Chloroplasts

38. Which of the following can be inferred from the information in the passage?

A) All cormorants exist in a juvenile stage with underdeveloped bone structures
B) The mutations on genes related to cilia caused the Galapagos cormorant to not be able to fly
C) Mouse cells and C. elegans are taken from the Galapagos cormorant bird
D) The Galapagos cormorant does not display a significant mutation in its genome

39. Which choice most effectively supports the answer to the previous question?

A) Lines 40-42 ("Cilia...people")
B) Lines 45-47 ("One...Burga")
C) Lines 51-53 ("Mutations...way")
D) Lines 54-58 ("They...research")

40. The word "persisted" in line 64 most nearly means:

A) Commemorated
B) Planned
C) Pressured
D) Continued

41. The final paragraph of the passage serves to:

A) Highlight a future implication that the study on Galapagos cormorants can have
B) Express a fault in the study done by Burga and his team
C) Pose a rhetorical question for the audience to ponder
D) Compare the inability for humans to fly to that of the Galapagos cormorant

42. The main idea of this passage is that

A) Burga and his team of researchers have discovered a new species of cormorant in the Galapagos
B) The Galapagos cormorant has a genetic mutation in the cilia gene
C) The Galapagos cormorant exhibits a unique evolutionary characteristic that poses many questions for scientists
D) The study of the Galapagos cormorant is unnecessary as Charles Darwin had already researched animals in the Galapagos Islands

Questions 1-10 are based on the following passage.

[1]

Ladies and gentlemen, tonight as we celebrate the one hundred forty-first birthday of one of the greatest men in American [1] history I would like to be able to talk about what a glorious day today is in the history of the world. As we celebrate the birth of this man who with his whole heart and soul hated war, I would like to be able to speak of peace in our time [2] —of war being outlawed— and of world-wide disarmament. These would be truly appropriate things to be able to [3] mention. As we celebrate the birthday of Abraham Lincoln.

[2]

[4] Five years after a world war has been won, men's hearts should anticipate a long peace—and men's minds should be free from the heavy weight that comes with war. But this is not such a period—for this is not a period of peace. This is a time of "the cold war." This is a time when the entire world is split into two vast, increasingly hostile armed camps—a time of a great armament race.

[3]

Today we can almost physically hear the mutterings and rumblings of an invigorated god of war. You can see it, feel it, and hear it all the way

1.

A) NO CHANGE
B) history; I
C) history: I
D) history, I

2.

A) NO CHANGE
B) : of war being outlawed:
C) "of war being outlawed"
D) —of war being outlawed:

3.

A) NO CHANGE
B) mention, as
C) mention: As
D) mention; as

4. At this point, the writer is considering adding the following sentence:

Sadly, peace in our time does not exist.

Should the writer make this addition here?

A) Yes, because it makes the audience feel emotional
B) Yes, because it introduces a contrasting idea presented in the paragraph
C) No, because it does not relate to the main idea of the passage
D) No, because peace is our time clearly exists

from the Indochina hills, from the shores of Formosa, right over into the very heart of Europe itself.

[4]

The one ⑤ encourage thing is that the "mad moment" has not yet arrived for the firing of the gun or the exploding of the bomb which will set civilization about the final task of destroying itself. There is still a hope for peace if we finally decide that no longer can we safely blind our eyes and close our ears to those facts which are shaping up more and more clearly, and that is that we are now engaged in a show-down fight, not the usual war between nations for land areas or other material gains, ⑥ and a war between two diametrically opposed ideologies.

[5]

The great difference between our western Christian world and the atheistic Communist world is not political, gentlemen, it is moral. For instance, the Marxian idea of ⑦ taking the land and factories and running the entire economy as a single enterprise is momentous. Likewise, Lenin's invention of the one-party police state as a way to make Marx's idea work is hardly less momentous.

[6]

Stalin's resolute putting across of these two ideas, of course, did much to divide the world. With only these differences, however, the east and the west could most certainly still live in peace.

5.
A) NO CHANGE
B) encouraged
C) encouragement
D) encouraging

6.
A) NO CHANGE
B) but
C) or
D) yet

7. The author wishes to use more complex vocabulary to express the underlined term. Which of the following best expresses the changes the author should make?

A) NO CHANGE
B) confiscating
C) steal
D) requiring

[7]

The real, basic difference, however, lies in the religion of immoralism . . . invented by Marx, preached feverishly by Lenin, and carried to unimaginable extremes by Stalin. This religion of immoralism, if the Red half of the world triumphs—and well it may, gentlemen—this religion of immoralism will more deeply 8 wound, hurt, and damage mankind than any conceivable economic or political system.

[8]

Karl Marx dismissed God as a hoax, and Lenin and Stalin have added in clear-cut, unmistakable language their resolve that no nation, no people who believe in a god, can exist side by side with their communistic state.

[9]

Today we are engaged in a final, all-out battle between communistic atheism and Christianity. The modern champions of communism 9 had selected this as the time, and ladies and gentlemen, the chips are down—they are truly down. 10

[10]

Karl Marx, for example, expelled people from his Communist Party for mentioning such things as love, justice, humanity or morality. He called this "soulful ravings" and "sloppy sentimentality."

8.

A) NO CHANGE
B) wound and damage and hurt
C) wound and hurt
D) wound

9.

A) NO CHANGE
B) are
C) have
D) having

10. For the sake of cohesion, paragraph 9 should be placed

A) NO CHANGE
B) after paragraph 6
C) after paragraph 7
D) after paragraph 10

Questions 11-20 are based on the following passage.

[11] Throughout its long history, Earth has warmed and cooled time and again. Climate has changed when the planet received more or less sunlight due to subtle shifts in its orbit, as the atmosphere or surface changed, or when the Sun's energy varied. But in the past century, another force has started to [12] influencing Earth's climate: humanity.

How does this warming compare to previous changes in Earth's climate? How can we be certain that human-released greenhouse gases are causing the warming? How much more will the Earth warm? How will Earth respond? Answering these questions is perhaps the most significant scientific challenge of our time. [13]

Global warming is the unusually rapid increase in Earth's average surface temperature over the past century primarily due to the greenhouse gases released as people burn fossil fuels. The global average surface temperature rose 0.6 to 0.9 degrees Celsius (1.1 to 1.6° F) between 1906 and 2005, and the rate of temperature increase has nearly doubled in the last 50 years. Surface temperatures are predicted to decrease in the future due to an ice age. [14]

11.

A) NO CHANGE
B) The Earth, throughout its long history, has warmed, time and cooled again
C) The Earth, throughout its long history, has warmed, time, and cooled again
D) The Earth has throughout its history warmed time and cooled again

12.

A) NO CHANGE
B) influenced
C) influence
D) influx

13. At this point the writer is considering adding the following sentence:

But first we must discover the causes and effects of global warming.

Should the writer make this addition here?

A) Yes, because it effectively leads into the next paragraph
B) Yes, because it is the main argument of the passage
C) No, because it contains unnecessary information
D) No, because the sentence does not relate to the main idea of the passage

Earth's temperature begins with the Sun. Roughly 30 percent of incoming sunlight is reflected back into space by bright surfaces like clouds and ice. Of the remaining 70 percent, most is absorbed by the land and ocean, and the rest is absorbed by the atmosphere. The absorbed solar energy heats our planet.

Global Mean Surface Temperatures (1900-2000)

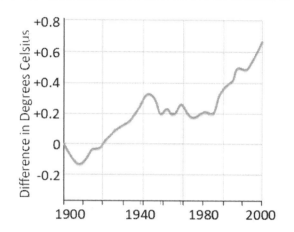

[15] As the rocks, the air and water, and the seas warm, they radiate "heat" energy (thermal infrared radiation). From the surface, this energy travels into the atmosphere where much of it is absorbed by water vapor and long-lived greenhouse gases such as carbon dioxide and methane.

When they absorb the energy radiating from Earth's surface, microscopic water or greenhouse gas molecules turn into tiny heaters— like the bricks in a fireplace, [16] they radiate heat even after the fire goes out. They radiate in all directions. The energy that radiates back toward Earth heats both the lower atmosphere and the

14. Based on the graph shown in the passage, which of the following would be the best revision of this sentence?

A) Global surface temperatures will continue to decrease for a few centuries
B) Global surface temperatures are likely to increase in the future
C) Global surface temperature is irrelevant in comparison to the ozone layer
D) Global surface temperature has been increasing for a few hundred years, but will continue the trend of decrease

15.

A) NO CHANGE
B) As the rocks air water and seas warm
C) As the air and water, and seas warm
D) As the rocks, air, water, and seas warm

16.

A) NO CHANGE
B) they radiate heat in all directions even after the fire goes out
C) they radiate in all directions heat even after out goes the fire
D) they radiate in all directions, inclusive of when the fire goes out in all directions

surface, enhancing the heating [17] they get from direct sunlight.

This absorption and radiation of heat by the atmosphere—the natural greenhouse effect—is [18] good for life on Earth. If there were no greenhouse effect, the Earth's average surface temperature would be a very chilly -18°C (0°F) instead of the comfortable 15°C (59°F) that it is today.

What has scientists concerned now is that over the past 250 years, humans have been artificially raising the concentration of greenhouse gases in [19] an atmosphere at an ever-increasing rate, mostly by burning fossil fuels, but also from cutting down carbon-absorbing forests. Since the Industrial Revolution began in about 1750, carbon dioxide levels have increased nearly 38 percent as of 2009 and methane levels have increased 148 percent.

[1] Since some of the extra energy from a warmer atmosphere radiates back down to the surface, Earth's surface temperature rises. [2] By increasing the concentration of greenhouse gases, we are making Earth's atmosphere a more efficient greenhouse. [3] The atmosphere today contains more greenhouse gas molecules, so more of the infrared energy emitted by the surface ends up being absorbed by the atmosphere. [20]

17. To improve the clarity of this sentence, the author should change the underlined word to:

A) NO CHANGE
B) it
C) energies
D) them

18. To make this sentence include a more complex variety of vocabulary, the author should change the underlined word to:

A) NO CHANGE
B) interesting
C) beneficial
D) malevolent

19.

A) NO CHANGE
B) a
C) the
D) they

20. For the sake of cohesion, sentence 3 should be placed :

A) NO CHANGE
B) Before sentence 1
C) After sentence 1
D) After sentence 2

Questions 21-30 are based on the following passage.

So let us begin anew--remembering on both sides that civility is not a sign of weakness, and sincerity is always subject to proof. Let us never negotiate out of 21 fear. But let us never fear to negotiate.

Let both sides explore what problems 22 united us instead of belaboring those problems which divide us.

Let both sides, for the first time, formulate serious and precise proposals for the inspection and control of 23 arms, and bring the absolute power to destroy other nations under the absolute control of all nations.

Let both sides seek to invoke the wonders of science instead of its terrors. Together let us explore the stars, conquer the deserts, eradicate disease, tap the ocean 24 depths and encourage the arts and commerce. 25

Let both sides unite to heed in all corners of the earth the command of Isaiah--to "undo the heavy burdens . . . (and) let the oppressed go free."

And if a beach-head of cooperation may push back the jungle of suspicion, let both sides join in

21.
A) NO CHANGE
B) fear, and
C) fear, or
D) fear, but

22.
A) NO CHANGE
B) uniting
C) will unite
D) unite

23.
A) NO CHANGE
B) arms, but
C) arms-and
D) arms: and

24.
A) NO CHANGE
B) depths, and
C) depths; and
D) depths, nor

25. At this point the writer is considering adding the following sentence:

I enjoy studying science and encourage everyone to study this subject

Should the writer make this addition here?

A) Yes, because it provides a context for the ideas stated in the previous sentence
B) Yes, because it provides emotional appeal for the audience
C) No, because this sentence does not relate to the main idea of the passage
D) No, because this sentence is not interesting for the audience

creating a new endeavor, not a new balance of power, but a new world of law, where the strong are just and the weak secure and the peace preserved.

All this will not be finished in the first one hundred days. Nor will it be finished in the first one thousand days, nor in the life of this Administration, nor even perhaps in our lifetime on this [26] planet. But let us begin.

In your hands, my fellow citizens, more than mine, will rest the final success or failure of our course. Since this country was [27] thought, each generation of Americans has been summoned to give testimony to its national loyalty. The graves of young Americans who answered the call to service surround the globe.

Now the trumpet summons us again-not as a call to bear arms, though arms we need [28] -not as a call to battle, though embattled we are-but a call to bear the burden of a long twilight struggle, year in and year out, "rejoicing in hope, patient in tribulation"--a struggle against the common enemies of man: tyranny, poverty, disease and war itself.

Can we forge against these enemies a grand and global alliance, North and South, East and West, that can assure a more fruitful life for all mankind? Will you join in that historic effort?

26. Which of the following most effectively combines the two sentences?

A) NO CHANGE
B) planet. but
C) planet, but
D) planet, and

27.

A) NO CHANGE
B) fought
C) revolutionized
D) founded

28.

A) NO CHANGE
B) : not as a call to battle, though embattled we are:
C) ; not as a call to battle, though embattled we are
D) "not as a call to battle, though embattled we are-

In the long history of the world, only a few generations have been granted the role of defending freedom in its hour of maximum danger. I do not shrink from this responsibility--I welcome it. I do not believe that any of us would exchange places with any other people or any other generation. [29] The energy, the faith, the devotion which we bring to this endeavor will light our country and all who serve it--and the glow from that fire can truly light the world.

And [30] so, my fellow Americans, ask not what your country can do for you--ask what you can do for your country.

29.

A) NO CHANGE
B) The energy, and faith, and devotion
C) The energy and faith and devotion
D) The energy, faith, and devotion

30.

A) NO CHANGE
B) so: my fellow Americans:
C) so, my fellow Americans;
D) so my fellow Americans

Questions 31-40 are based on the following passage.

[31] Plastic shopping bags are incredibly cheap and useful, their disposal causes widespread pollution. That's because the non-biodegradable polyethylene takes centuries to decompose and is also detrimental to wildlife who often mistake the colorful debris for food. Now, we [32] had an unlikely ally to help clean up our trash – a small wax worm bred primarily for use as premium fish bait.

Federica Bertocchini, a developmental biologist at the Spanish National Research Council, stumbled upon the grub's hidden skills by accident. About two years ago, the amateur beekeeper was cleaning out her hives that had become infested with the Galleria mellonella, or honeycomb moth, caterpillars. The larvae are the bane of beekeepers worldwide because of their voracious appetite for the wax that bees use to build honeycombs. [33]

The researcher [34] says "I removed the worms and put them in a plastic bag while I cleaned the panels. After finishing, I went back to the room where I had left the worms, and I found that they were everywhere. They had escaped from the bag even though it had been closed and when I checked, I saw that the bag was full of holes. There was only one explanation: the worms had made the holes and had escaped."

31. The author wants to add a transition word to convey contrast. Which of the following is the best word to insert at this point in the passage?

A) NO CHANGE
B) Although
C) However
D) Additionally

32.

A) NO CHANGE
B) have had
C) having
D) have

33. Which choice serves most effectively as the main topic of this paragraph?

A) There is no main topic
B) Development biologist Bertocchini discovered the abilities of a wax-eating larvae
C) Bertocchini was considered the bane of beekeepers worldwide
D) Galleria mellonella are the most important larvae in the insect world

34.

A) NO CHANGE
B) says, I
C) says, "I
D) says: "I

Realizing she may have stumbled upon an important discovery, Bertocchini teamed up with Paolo Bombelli and Christopher Howe from Cambridge University to conduct further research. They began by placing 100 worms on some polyethylene. [35] Over a 24-hour period, the worms managed to gnaw through 92 milligrams of plastic. The researchers estimate that at this rate, the group of worms could decompose an average-sized 5.5-gram plastic bag within a month.

To [36] ruling out the possibility that chewing was causing the degradation, the researchers spread the soft pulp of some recently deceased worms on a sheet of plastic. Sure enough, even the liquid larvae were able to eat through the material, confirming that the worms have a plastic-digesting enzyme. Further tests revealed that the only residue left behind was ethylene glycol, a biodegradable chemical compound commonly used in antifreeze. The researchers believe that the worm's ability to digest plastic is a coincidence and stems from its diet of beeswax that comprises the same carbon bonds as polyethylene.

35. At this point the writer is considering adding the following sentence:

The scientists discovered that each was able to create about 2.2 holes per hour.

Should the writer make this addition here?

A) Yes, because this provides crucial information about the results of the experiment
B) Yes, because this establishes the main idea of the passage
C) No, because this statement is irrelevant to the passage
D) No, because this passage includes a personal statement of opinion

36.

A) NO CHANGE
B) rule
C) ruled
D) will rule

While the news is certainly encouraging, not everyone is convinced the grubs can help reduce our ever-growing mountains of trash. [37] University of Michigan's Ramani Narayan believes the tiny pieces of microplastics released by the plastic-eating caterpillars would pick up toxins and transport them up the food chain, causing, even more, harm to the environment and human health. The skeptical researcher quips, "Biodegradation isn't a magical solution to plastics waste management."

Susan Selke, director of Michigan State University School of Packaging, is concerned that the caterpillars will not be able to survive in an oxygen-free landfill environment. Additionally, it is unclear if the worms are chewing through the plastic to escape or because it provides them with energy. According to Bombelli, "If they just want to escape, they are going to get fed up very [38] soon. But if they're munching it to use as an energy source it's a completely different ball game. We are not yet able to answer this, but we're working on it."

However, Bertocchini is not planning to deploy worm armies to landfills. Instead, the researcher wants to identify the enzyme that helps degrade the plastic. The researcher says, "Maybe we can find the molecule and produce it at high-scale, rather than using a million worms in a plastic bag." This is not the first time scientists have discovered

37. Which of the following statements should the author include at this point in the passage in reference to the graph shown in the article?

A) The per capita beverage bottle waste has increased eight-fold from 1990 to 2006
B) The per capita beverage bottle waste has decreased from 1990 to 2006
C) The per capita beverage bottle waste has increased at a very slow rate in the past 100 years
D) The per capita beverage bottle waste is rising at a much faster rate than the per capita food waste

38. Which of the following effectively combines the two sentences?

A) NO CHANGE
B) soon but
C) soon, but
D) soon; but

wax worms that eat human-generated trash. In 2014, a team from China's Beihang University discovered that the larvae of Indian meal moths, the most common pantry pests, also consume plastic. However, the bacteria in the wax 39 worm's stomachs took much longer to digest the material then Bertocchini's worms. Then, in 2015, the Chinese researchers collaborated with scientists from California's Stanford University to investigate mealworms that enjoy eating Styrofoam. Whether any of these organisms are strong enough to help 40 move our trash remains to be seen.

Meanwhile, the only way to solve this self-inflicted problem is by reducing plastic bag usage — so be sure to always carry a recyclable bag with you.

39.

A) NO CHANGE
B) worms
C) worm's
D) worms'

40.

A) NO CHANGE
B) eliminate
C) transfer
D) cancel

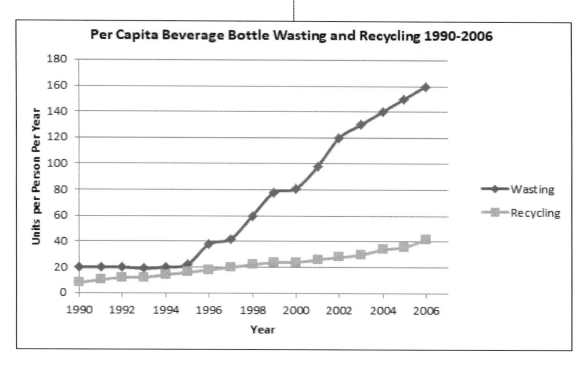

DIRECTIONS

For questions 1-9, solve each problem and choose the best answer from the choices provided. Fill in the corresponding circle on your answer sheet. For questions 10-13, solve the problem and bubble in your answer on the grid provided.

NOTES

- Calculator is **NOT allowed** in this section
- All variables and expressions represent real numbers unless otherwise indicated
- All figures are drawn to scale unless otherwise stated
- All figures lie in the same plane unless otherwise stated
- The domain of a given function is the set of all real numbers, unless otherwise stated

REFERENCE

$A = \pi r^2$

$C = 2\pi r$

$A = l \cdot w$

$A = \dfrac{bh}{2}$

$V = lwh$

$V = \pi r^2 h$

$a^2 + b^2 = c^2$

Special Right Triangles

1. If $B = x \cdot y$, then $2x \cdot 5y =$

A) $2B$
B) $3B$
C) $5B$
D) $10B$

2. After 6 gallons of water are poured into a tank, $\frac{1}{12}$ of it is filled. What is the total water capacity of this tank?

A) 12 gallons
B) 24 gallons
C) 48 gallons
D) 72 gallons

3. The ratio of boys to girls in a classroom is 3:2. If there are a total of 30 children in the class, how many of them are girls?

A) 12
B) 15
C) 18
D) 21

4. If $\frac{x}{4} + \frac{x}{3} = \frac{7}{12}$, then $x =$

A) 0
B) 1
C) 3
D) 12

5.

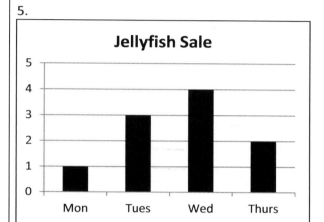

The bar graph above shows the number of new jellyfish sold at a pet shop. If each jellyfish costs $2.25, then how much money did the pet shop make on jellyfish during the four day period?

A) $20.25
B) $22.50
C) $24.75
D) $225.00

6. A car salesman receives a salary of 5000 dollars a month plus a 50% commission of his monthly car sales in dollars. If his total compensation in September was $10,000, what is the value of the cars that he sold?

A) 5000
B) 10,000
C) 15,000
D) 20,000

7. At a certain grocery store, 1 orange and 2 apples cost $5.00 while 3 oranges and 4 apples cost $11.00. What is the cost of 1 orange?

A) $0.50
B) $0.75
C) $1.00
D) $1.50

8. Which of the following points (x, y) satisfies the inequality $x < 5y + 2$?

A) $(2, -4)$
B) $(2, 0)$
C) $(2, 2)$
D) $(4, 0)$

9. How many integer solutions does the inequality $|2x + 5| < 10$ have?

A) 9
B) 10
C) 11
D) 12

10. The expression $(2x + 1)(x + 2)$ can also be expressed as which of the following?

A) $2x + 5 + 2$
B) $2x^2 + 5x$
C) $3x + 3$
D) $2x^2 + 5x + 2$

11. A taxi cab charges a flat rate of $25.00 and an additional 25 cents for each mile. How many miles would a passenger need to travel to have a taxi fare of $75?

GRID IN

13. How many points of intersection do the graphs of $y = |5x + 2|$ and $y = -12$ have?

GRID IN

12. What value of c makes the following system have an infinite number of solutions?

$$4x + 8y = 3$$
$$8x + 16y = c$$

GRID IN

DIRECTIONS

For questions 1-21, solve each problem and choose the best answer from the choices provided. Fill in the corresponding circle on your answer sheet. For questions 22-25, solve the problem and bubble in your answer on the grid provided.

NOTES

- Calculator **is allowed** in this section
- All variables and expressions represent real numbers unless otherwise indicated
- All figures are drawn to scale unless otherwise stated
- All figures lie in the same plane unless otherwise stated
- The domain of a given function is the set of all real numbers, unless otherwise stated

REFERENCE

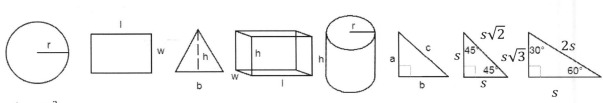

$A = \pi r^2$

$C = 2\pi r$

$A = l \cdot w$ $A = \dfrac{bh}{2}$ $V = lwh$ $V = \pi r^2 h$ $a^2 + b^2 = c^2$ Special Right Triangles

1. If $2^n = 32$, what is the value of n^2?

A) 16
B) 25
C) 49
D) 64

2. Which of the following ordered pairs is a solution for the linear equation given below?

$$y = \frac{5}{2}x + 7$$

A) (1,2.5)
B) (1,7.5)
C) (1,9.5)
D) (1,11.5)

3. The prime factorization of 132 is:

A) 2^7
B) $2^3 \cdot 3^2$
C) $2^2 \cdot 3 \cdot 7$
D) $2^2 \cdot 3 \cdot 11$

4. If 3 men can cut a lawn in 6 hours, how many men are needed to cut the same lawn in 3 hours?

A) 6
B) 12
C) 18
D) 24

5. In a certain container, temperature in kelvin (K) and pressure in atmospheres (atm) are directly proportional. When the container has a temperature of 300K, it has a pressure of 1 atm. What is the temperature of the container when the pressure is doubled?

A) 150K
B) 300K
C) 450K
D) 600K

6. What percent of 200 is 50?

A) 12.5%
B) 25%
C) 50%
D) 75%

8. Which of the following is a solution to the absolute inequality shown below?

$$\left|\frac{4}{3}(x+3)\right| = 8$$

A) -9
B) -2
C) -3
D) 9

7. There are 100 centimeters in a meter, and 1000 meters in a kilometer. How many centimeters are in a kilometer?

A) 1,000
B) 100,000
C) 1,000,000
D) 10,000,000

Set A: {3,4,5,5,5,5,6,7 }

9. What is the sum of the mean, median, and mode for the set of numbers shown above?

A) 13
B) 14
C) 14.5
D) 15

10. How many 7 digit phone numbers can be created starting with the number 5 and ending with the number 3? Assume that numbers can be repeated.

A) 100
B) 1,000
C) 10,000
D) 100,000

11. The probability that a person is born with blue eyes is 2%. Out of 150 people who are born in a certain hospital, how many have blue eyes?

A) 2
B) 3
C) 4
D) 5

12. If $-223 \leq 15x + 2 < 152$, then which of the following CANNOT be the solution of this inequality?

A) -15
B) 0
C) 7
D) 10

13. If $f(x) = x^2 + 2$ and $g(x) = 2x - 2$, then $(f + g)(x) =$

A) $x^2 + 2x + 4$
B) $x^2 + 2x - 2$
C) $2x^3$
D) $x^2 + 2x$

14. Solve the following equation for x:
$$\sqrt{3x + 1} = \sqrt{2x}$$

A) -1
B) 0
C) 1
D) No solution

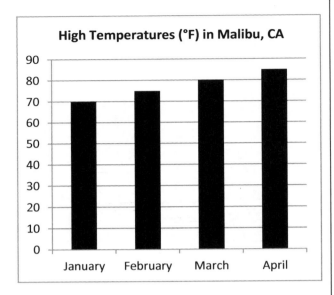

High Temperatures (°F) in Malibu, CA

The table below shows the results of a survey of 216 people regarding the language that they speak at home.

	English	French	Spanish	Total
0-10	10	5	10	25
11-20	21	8	2	31
21-30	35	2	11	48
31+	75	12	25	112
Total	141	27	48	216

15. The graph above shows the high temperature average for four months in Malibu, California. Which of the following best describes the trend in the values of high temperatures?

A) Parabolic
B) Linear
C) Cubic
D) Non-Linear

17. Based on the table above, what it the probability that a person speaks English at home?

A) $\frac{141}{216}$

B) $\frac{75}{216}$

C) $\frac{36}{216}$

D) $\frac{112}{216}$

16. If Tom drives his car for 7 hours at a speed of 66 miles per hour and then 10 hours at a speed of 85 miles per hour, what is his average speed in miles per hour during the 17 hours of driving? Round to the nearest tenths place.

A) 75.5
B) 77.2
C) 78.5
D) 84.5

18. Based on the table shown above, what is the probability that a child aged 0-10 speaks Spanish?

A) 20%
B) 30%
C) 40%
D) 75%

19. A ball bounces vertically several times. After the first bounce, it reaches a height of 81 centimeters. For the next bounce, it reaches a height of 27 centimeters. For the 3rd bounce, it reaches a height of 9 centimeters. Which of the following models best describes this scenario where h is the height reached and x is the number of times the ball has bounced?

A) $h = 81 \cdot \left(\frac{1}{3}\right)^{x-1}$

B) $h = 81 \cdot \left(\frac{1}{3}\right)^{x}$

C) $h = \left(\frac{1}{3}\right)^{x}$

D) $h = \left(\frac{1}{3}\right)x$

20. The number of adult (a) and child (c) tickets sold must total more than 50, and the total revenue from the ticket sales must be greater than or equal to \$400. If adult tickets cost \$3 and child tickets cost \$2, which of the following systems models this scenario?

A) $a + c > 50$
   $2a + 3c < 400$

B) $a + c < 50$
   $2a + 3c \geq 400$

C) $a + c > 50$
   $3a + 2c \geq 400$

D) $a + c = 50$
   $3a + 2c \geq 400$

21. If $x\sqrt{2} + 3 = \sqrt{17}$, then what is the value of x? Round to the nearest hundredths digit.

A) 0.79
B) 0.81
C) 5.04
D) 5.05

22. A motorcycle starts off at rest. The velocity of a motorcycle increases by 2 meters per second every second for 60 seconds. After this, the velocity decreases at a rate of 10 meters per second every second for 4 seconds. What is the final velocity, in meters per second, of the motorcycle?

GRID IN

24. Bank A offers compounded interest of 3% on an investment, whereas Bank B offers a simple interest of 300 dollars a year to an investment. If $1000 is deposited in both banks, what will be the difference in amounts in the two banks after 5 years? Round your answer to the nearest whole dollar.

GRID IN

25. The ratio of blue marbles to green marbles in a bag is 1:3. The ratio of green marbles to red marbles in the bag is 6:3. The ratio of red to black marbles in the bag is 27:7. What is the least number of marbles that the bag can have?

GRID IN

23. What is the sum of the coefficients of the variables of $(2x + 1)(2x + 2)$ when it is expressed in standard form?

GRID IN

PRACTICE TEST 1 - ANSWERS- READING TEST

#	Explanation
1 D	In lines 1-4, the excerpt states that Mary "was the most disagreeable-looking child ever seen." Answer choices A, B, and C deal with the taste of a certain food, whereas answer choice D correctly describes the personality of Mary.
2 C	The passage states that "her face was yellow because she had been born in India and had always been ill in one way or another." This shows that the direct causation for her face being yellow was the fact that she was born in India and was very sick, making answer choice C correct.
3 B	The passage clearly states that Mary's mother "had not wanted a little girl at all" and wanted to "keep the child out of sight as much as possible," making answer choice B the correct inference.
4 C	The best support for the inference that Mary's mother did not like her child is found in lines 14-19, where the passage states Mary's mother "had not wanted a little girl" and that she wanted to "keep the child out of sight," answer choice C.
5 A	Lines 29-31 state "by the time she was six years old she was as tyrannical and selfish a little pig as ever lived," making a direct comparison between Mary and a little pig. A simile makes a direct comparison using the words "like" or "as," meaning that a simile is used in this sentence, answer choice A.
6 B	The passage states that "The young English governess who came to teach her to read and write..." This means that a governess is a kind of teacher, answer choice B.
7 A	Lines 50-51 of the passage state "Mary threw herself into a passion and beat and kicked her," showing that Mary wishes to get her way no matter what. This indicates that Mary can be best described as a spoiled child, answer choice A.
8 D	The last paragraph uses words such as "mysterious," "missing," and "scared," to show that there is a conflict in Maya's story that involves suspense, answer choice D.
9 A	Lines 11-14 state that "whether this nation, born of a declaration that all men were created with an equal right to liberty, would continue to exist as the largest slaveholding country in the world." This explains the contrast between the declaration that all men are created equal and the fact that slaveholding still existed in the US, implying that not everyone had equal liberties during this time, answer choice A.
10 C	Lines 18-19 state "But these achievements..." meaning that the author believes that the Civil War resulted in several positive achievements for the winning side, answer choice C.
11 C	Lines 15-19 state "Northern victory in the war preserved the United States as one nation and ended the institution of slavery that had divided the country from its beginning. But these achievements came at the cost..." This best supports the idea that the Civil War had a positive outcome and was a good achievement, answer choice C

12 D	The word uncompromising means unable to reach a decision or an agreement. This is usually between two people who are not flexible to change their ideas. The opposite of flexible is inflexible, answer choice D.
13 B	The passage states that "The incoming Lincoln administration and most of the Northern people refused to recognize the legitimacy of secession. They feared that it would discredit democracy and create a fatal precedent that would eventually fragment the no-longer United States into several small, squabbling countries." This quote explains that Lincoln and his administration did not want to see the Union split apart due to secession, and did not support the fragmentation of the US, answer choice B.
14 C	The word triggered is used in this sentence to indicate the beginning of the war, meaning the event at Fort Sumter "started" the war, answer choice C.
15 D	Paragraph 4 begins with a discussion of the first event of the Civil War, the battle at Fort Sumter. The paragraph continues to discuss events until the end of 1861. This means that the paragraph is giving a summary of events towards the beginning of the Civil War, answer choice D.
16 C	The author speaks throughout the passage as a narrator with a complete understanding of the situation, including the causes and effects of the Civil War. Since the narrator knows all of the events that took place, the point of view is third person omniscient, answer choice C.
17 A	The main idea of the passage is that the Civil War was the "central event in America's historical consciousness," and determined the future of the country. This most nearly correlates to answer choice A, that the Civil War had a lasting impact on American History.
18 A	As used in line 6, the black holes are being described as joining together to create a larger black hole. This means that the black holes are combining together, answer choice A.
19 C	Paragraph 2 states that "such a dramatic merger may seem alarming..." implying that the public may be scared of the black hole collision, answer choice C.
20 C	Lines 7-9 states that the collision of the black holes "may seem alarming." These lines support the fact that the public may be fearful of the black hole collision, answer choice C.
21 B	The passage states that black hole observations are "analyzed by an international collaboration," which are located in places like Washington and Louisiana. This idea best correlates to answer choice B.
22 A	To easily answer this question look for context clues. The previous sentence states "LIGO detected gravitational waves for the first time in history." This means that a ripple is a kind of wave that the system has detected, answer choice A.
23 D	The passage states that "Pairs of black holes not only spiral around each other; they also spin individually on their own axes," eliminating answer choices A and C. Additionally, in lines 5-6 the passage states "But when they merged, they created a monster," meaning that answer

	choice B is also a true statement. This leaves answer choice D to be the correct answer, as this fact is never stated anywhere in the passage.
24 A	The main idea of the passage is the study of two black holes that coexist near each other. This idea is stated in the first paragraph with the discussion of the combining stars as well as in the last paragraph, which discusses the impact of the study of binary black holes. The overall discussion of black hole collision deals with the study of binary black holes, answer choice A.
25 C	The best way to answer this question is through the process of elimination. The diagram shows that the final stage of a massive star is either a black hole or a neutron star. This means that the final stage of the sun cannot be a black hole or a neutron star, making answer choices A and B incorrect. Furthermore, the diagram shows that the supernova is the second to last stage of a massive star, meaning that it cannot be the last stage of an average star like the Sun. This means that answer choice C is the only possible choice.
26 B	In lines 1-6, the author uses phrases like "any man with a heart" and "agree with me" to make the audience support his argument. This rhetorical strategy can best be described as persuasion, answer choice B.
27 D	In lines 8-11, the author states "all the ills of present-day society, which is normally attributed to the imperfection of human nature, is in fact the lack of organization of human society." This means that the author believes that human society has a few problems that he thinks are like illnesses, answer choice D.
28 B	The author repeatedly states that he supports communism through phrases like "The idea of communism, gentlemen, with which everyone says he agrees, is the life-law of love applied to social life," and "concerning the possibility of realizing communism and the fundamental cause of human miseries..." These phrases show that the author supports communism as a viable solution for society, answer choice B.
29 D	Senator McCarthy uses lines 16-20 to show that the influence of communism has increased significantly, overshadowing the control of the United States. He states that "the odds have changed" in favor of the Soviet Union, expressing the idea that the Soviet Union is defeating the United States, answer choice D.
30 B	The word tempo, as it is used in this sentence, relates to the speed, or rate, of Communist victories over the United States. This means that the word tempo most nearly means rate, answer choice B.
31 A	In this sentence, McCarthy states that the destruction of the US government will be caused by "enemies from within." With this statement, McCarthy is accusing members of the US government of being communists, answer choice A.
32 A	The diagram shows that capitalism gained popularity at a much faster rate than communism, supporting the capitalistic ideas of McCarthy, answer choice A

33 C	In this question, we are looking for the false statement. The fact that the author of excerpt 1 would support the argument of excerpt 2 is a false statement, since excerpt 1 supports communism whereas excerpt 2 does not support communism, answer choice C.
34 A	In Hess's speech, he states that communism can fix the "lack of organization of human society," while McCarthy completely rejects the ideas of communism. This means that only McCarthy would support the idea that communism does not generate a perfect society, answer choice A.
35 D	The passage states that only one species of cormorant on the Galapagos islands cannot fly, causing scientists to research this specific species, answer choice D.
36 D	The passage states that there is a "short evolutionary distance between Galapagos cormorants and other species... ideal candidates for looking at genetic changes." This means that the evolutionary distance refers to the changes in the evolutionary biology of a certain species over many years, answer choice D.
37 A	The word genome in line 35 relates to the "distinct mutation found around genes" in the cormorant. This means that genome most nearly means the genes of an organism, answer choice A.
38 B	The passage states that the mutation in the cilia genes caused the skeletal structure of the Galapagos cormorant to have a juvenile structure, preventing it from flying, answer choice B.
39 C	Lines 51-53 state that "Mutations on genes related to cilia or skeletal growth could help change the birds' skeletal structure in this way." This provides evidence to the fact that the mutation in the cilia gene caused the birds' skeletal structure to be deformed, causing it to lose the ability to fly, answer choice C.
40 D	Lines 63-64 state "So why would this mutation have persisted in the Galapagos population?" We know from the rest of the passage/context clues that this mutation is still present in the Galapagos cormorant. This means that the mutation continues to exist, answer choice D.
41 A	The final paragraph discusses parallels between the study of the evolution of the Galapagos cormorant to the evolution of humans, and hints at a future study comparing humans and cormorants, answer choice A.
42 C	The main idea of the passage, as seen towards the beginning, is that the Galapagos cormorant is not able to fly, and that this specific evolutionary trait is being studied by scientists. Additionally, the passage poses many questions that come up based on the research done by scientists on this species of cormorant, answer choice C.

PRACTICE TEST 1 – ANSWERS – WRITING AND LANGUAGE TEST

#	Explanation
1 D	The speaker uses the phrase "tonight as we celebrate the one hundred forty-first birthday of one of the greatest men in American history" as a description of the event. Since this information is an interjection, a comma is the best punctuation to use to separate the clauses of this sentence, answer choice D.
2 A	When a hyphen is used in the middle of a sentence, it needs a second hyphen to enclose the information it contains. This means that there needs to be a hyphen before and after the phrase "of war being outlawed," answer choice A.
3 B	The best punctuation to effectively combine these two sentences is a comma. Since a colon is used to introduce a list, and a semi colon is used to separate two independent clauses, a comma is the most effective punctuation in this situation, answer choice B.
4 B	The main idea of paragraph 2 is that the Cold War has caused the war to continue, meaning that peace in our time does not exist. The addition of this sentence would help set up the introduction of the period of existing war mentioned in the paragraph, answer choice B.
5 D	This sentence is spoken in the future/present tense. This means that the answer choice must be in the progressive tense (with an –ing at the end of the word), answer choice D.
6 B	This sentence uses two clauses that are contrasting. The first clause states that the war is "not the usual war between nations for land areas or other material gains," and the second clause states "a war between two diametrically opposed ideologies." This means that the contrasting word that should be used between these sentences is "but," answer choice B.
7 B	A synonym for the word "taking" is "confiscating". The usage of the word "confiscating" makes the passage have a more complex and articulate vocabulary that adds meaning to the passage, answer choice B.
8 D	The best way to make this sentence flow smoothly is to remove unnecessary synonyms in the sentence. Since wound/hurt/damage all mean almost the same thing, we can just use one of these words in the sentence, answer choice D.
9 C	Paragraph 9 is spoken in the present tense, as seen in the first sentence. This means the verb "had" needs to be converted to the present tense, or "have," answer choice C.
10 D	Paragraph 9 is a conclusion, as the speaker provides a summary of the argument and ends with a strong idiom. This means that the paragraph should be placed at the end of the passage, or after paragraph 10, answer choice D
11 A	The sentence does not need revision as it correctly uses a comma to separate the two clauses in the sentence, answer choice A.
12 C	The word influencing must be changed to the present tense to match with the phrase "has started." The only option is "influence," answer choice C.

13 A	This sentence provides a good transition to the next paragraph, which is a discussion of global warming on earth, answer choice A.
14 B	The graph shows that the global surface temperatures have been on a steady increase since around 1900. This means that the temperatures are likely to increase in the future, answer choice B.
15 D	In a list of words, there should be a comma after every word. This is best seen in answer choice D, where a list of objects is shown in the proper formatting.
16 B	To make the flow of the sentence more precise, the description of how the heat radiates can placed in the previous sentence as shown in answer choice B. This makes the description of the radiation of heat more concise for the reader.
17 A	None of the answer choices provided help improve the clarity of the sentence. The word "they" is used to describe the lower atmosphere/surface mentioned in the first clause of the sentence, answer choice A.
18 C	A better synonym for the word "good" is "beneficial." This word makes the sentence more complex and improves the overall message, answer choice C.
19 C	The word "an" is used before the word "atmosphere." Since there is only one atmosphere on the Earth, the word "the" should be used instead, answer choice C.
20 B	Sentence 3 is an introductory sentence. Additionally, sentence 1 serves as an extension of sentence 3, meaning that sentence 3 should be placed before sentence 1, answer choice B.
21 D	The most effective way to combine these two sentences is to use a comma and the word "but" in lowercase, answer choice D.
22 D	The sentence is written in the present/future tense. This means that the verb "united" cannot be in the past tense, and thus must be in the present tense. The choice that works best in this sentence is "unite," answer choice D.
23 A	The ", and" effectively combines the two complex sentences together and does not need further revision, answer choice A.
24 B	A comma must be placed before the word "and" since the sentence includes a list. A list is always in the form (A, B, C, and D). Notice the comma after the C. This makes answer choice B the correct syntax for this sentence.
25 C	The main idea of the passage deals with patriotism and uniting the country. It would not be appropriate for the writer to include a personal opinion and lose his formal tone, answer choice C.
26 C	To effectively combine these two sentences, replace the period with a comma and make the word "but" lowercase. This will allow the sentences to flow together properly, answer choice C.

27 D	This sentence refers to the past history of the country. This means that the word "thought" should be replaced with the word "founded" to indicate the continuity of the loyalty mentioned in the sentence, answer choice D.
28 A	The hyphens in this sentence are already used in the correct format, located before and after the interjectory phrase, answer choice A.
29 D	The items in this list can best be separated using commas. Additionally the repeated word "the" can be removed for each item in the list. The best condensed form of this sentence is answer choice D.
30 A	The interjection "my fellow Americans" is best contained using two commas. Thus, the sentence does not require any revision, answer choice A.
31 B	The word "although," when inserted at the beginning of the passage, provides sufficient contrast to make the two clauses of the sentence contrast, answer choice B.
32 D	The sentence is written in the present tense. This means that the word "had" needs to be converted into the present tense as well. The flow of the sentence is best written using the word "have," answer choice D.
33 B	This paragraph details how biologist Federica Bertocchini discovered plastic-eating larvae by accident while tending her beehives. This most closely matches with the wording of answer choice B.
34 C	Before the start of a quoted phrase, a comma is always necessary. This means that answer choice C is the only grammatically correct format of this phrase.
35 A	This sentence provides the results of the scientists' experiment on plastic eating worms. This means that it is a crucial piece of information that is relevant to the passage, answer choice A.
36 B	The sentence uses the word "spread" later on, indicating that the sentence is written in the past tense. This means that "ruling" must be changed from present progressive to a form of the past tense. The answer choice that best replaces the underlined word is "rule," answer choice B.
37 A	The graph shows an increase in the per capita waste from 20 in 1990 to 160 in 2006. This means that the per capita beverage bottle waste has increased eight-fold from 1990 to 2006, answer choice A.
38 C	To effectively combine the sentences, there needs to be a comma before the word "but." This means that the only correct answer is C.
39 D	The sentence is referring to worms in the plural form as seen in the previous sentence. This means that the word must be changed to the plural possessive form, or "worms'," answer choice D.
40 B	The sentence states that the organisms are needed to be very strong. This means that strong organisms have the ability to remove or eliminate trash remains, answer choice B.

PRACTICE TEST 1 – ANSWERS – MATH TEST-No Calculator

#	Explanation
1 D	We can rewrite the expression $2x \cdot 5y$ as $2 \cdot x \cdot 5 \cdot y$. Since multiplication is a commutative property, the numbers in the expression can be rearranged. This means that $$2 \cdot x \cdot 5 \cdot y = 2 \cdot 5 \cdot x \cdot y$$ $$= 10 \cdot x \cdot y$$ We were given that $B = x \cdot y$. Therefore substituting B into the expression above for $x \cdot y$ gives: $$2x \cdot 5y = 10B$$
2 D	If 6 gallons of water fill up $\frac{1}{12}$ of the tank, that means that the tank can hold 12 times this amount. Thus, $6 \cdot 12 = 72 \ gallons$.
3 A	The ratio given means that there are 3 boys in the class for every 2 girls. This means that for every 5 children, 2 of them are girls and 3 of them are boys. Since there are a total of 30 children in the class, $\frac{2}{5}$ of them are girls. $$\frac{2}{5} \cdot 30 = 12 \ girls$$
4 B	$$\frac{x}{4} + \frac{x}{3} = \frac{7}{12}$$ $$\frac{3x + 4x}{12} = \frac{7}{12}$$ $$\frac{7x}{12} = \frac{7}{12}$$ $$84x = 84$$ $$x = 1$$
5 B	According to the bar graph, 1 jellyfish was sold on Monday, 3 were sold on Tuesday, 4 were sold on Wednesday, and 2 were sold on Thursday. This gives a total of $$1 + 3 + 4 + 2 = 10 \ jellyfish$$ Since each jelly fish was sold for $2.25, the total sales is equal to $$2.25 \cdot 10 = \$22.50$$

6 B	The salesman received a total of $10,000 in compensation. Since his base salary is $5000, and he receives 50% of his car sales (x), the value of his car sales can be found using the equation:
	$$5000 + 0.5x = 10000$$ $$0.5x = 5000$$ $$x = \frac{5000}{0.5} = \$10000$$
7 C	Let $x = oranges$ and $y = apples$:
	$$1x + 2y = 5$$ $$3x + 4y = 11$$ Solving by substituting gives: $$x = 5 - 2y$$ $$3(5 - 2y) + 4y = 11$$ $$15 - 6y + 4y = 11$$ $$15 - 2y = 11$$ $$2y = 4$$ $$y = \$2$$ Since we have found out that apples cost 2 dollars, each, we can plug this value back into one of the original equations above: $$1x + 2(2) = 5$$ $$x = \$1$$
8 C	The best way to answer this question is to plug in all the answer choices into the inequality given. A) $2 < 5(-4) + 2 \rightarrow 2 < -18$ FALSE B) $2 < 5(0) + 2 \rightarrow 2 < 2$ FALSE C) $2 < 5(2) + 2 \rightarrow 2 < 12$ TRUE D) $4 < 5(0) + 2 \rightarrow 4 < 2$ FALSE

9 B	The absolute value inequality can be rewritten as:
	$$-10 < 2x + 5 < 10$$
	This simplifies to:
	$$-15 < 2x < 5$$
	$$-7.5 < x < 2.5$$
	The integer solutions are: -7,-6,-5,-4,-3,-2,-1,0,1, and 2. This is a total of 10 integer solutions.
10 D	To expand this expression, we can use the FOIL method:
	$$(2x + 1)(x + 2) = 2x \cdot x + 4x + x + 2$$
	$$2x^2 + 5x + 2$$
11 200	Since there is a flat rate of 25 dollars, the total mileage cost for the passenger is 75-25=$50.00. Since one mile equals 25 cents, the number of miles traveled equals
	$$\frac{5000}{25} = \frac{1000}{5} = 200 \; miles$$
12 6	Remember that for a system to have an infinite number of solutions, they must be the exact same line. We can multiply all of the terms in the first equation by a factor of two to get the following
	$$2(4x + 8y = 3)$$
	$$8x + 16y = 6$$
	This means that if $c = 6$, then both equations will be of the exact same line, thus having an infinite number of solutions.
13 0	The absolute value bars in an equation make the function inside them positive. This means that the graph of $y = |5x + 2|$ always has positive values. Therefore, it can never be equal to -12. This means that there are 0 points of intersection.

PRACTICE TEST 1 – ANSWERS – MATH TEST- Calculator

#	Explanation
1 B	32 can be rewritten as 2^5. This means that $n = 5$, and $n^2 = 25$.
2 C	The answer choices all provide the x coordinate as 1. This means that $x = 1$ can be plugged into the linear equation to get a y-value. $$y = \frac{5}{2}(1) + 7$$ $$y = 2.5 + 7$$ $$y = 9.5$$ This makes the ordered pair that satisfies the equation $(1, 9.5)$.
3 D	132 equals $2 \cdot 66$. 132 equals $2 \cdot 3 \cdot 22$. 132 equals $2 \cdot 3 \cdot 2 \cdot 11$ Since 11 is a prime number and cannot be broken down further, the prime factorization of 132 is $2^2 \cdot 3 \cdot 11$
4 A	If 3 men take 6 hours to cut the lawn, twice as many men are needed to cut the lawn in half the time, since the two variables are inversely proportional. This means that 6 men are needed to cut the lawn in 3 hours.
5 D	The problem states that temperature and pressure are directly proportional. This means that if temperature increases, so does the pressure. At a temperature of $300K$, the pressure is $1\ atm$. At twice the pressure, $2\ atm$, the temperature is $2 \cdot 300K = 600K$.
6 B	This can be expressed as the fraction $\frac{50}{200}$. This simplifies to $\frac{1}{4}$. Expressed as a percentage, $\frac{1}{4} = 25\%$.
7 B	$$\frac{100\ centimeters}{1\ \cancel{meter}} \cdot \frac{1000\ \cancel{meters}}{1\ kilometer}$$ $$100 \cdot 1000 = 100,000\ centimeters\ per\ kilometer$$

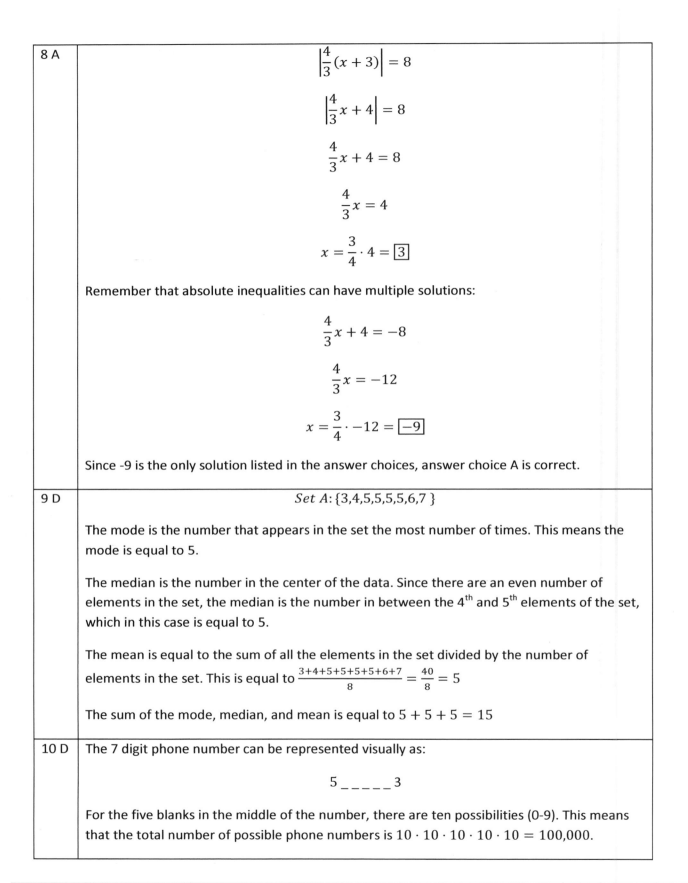

8 A	$$\left|\frac{4}{3}(x+3)\right| = 8$$
	$$\left|\frac{4}{3}x+4\right| = 8$$
	$$\frac{4}{3}x+4 = 8$$
	$$\frac{4}{3}x = 4$$
	$$x = \frac{3}{4}\cdot 4 = \boxed{3}$$
	Remember that absolute inequalities can have multiple solutions:
	$$\frac{4}{3}x+4 = -8$$
	$$\frac{4}{3}x = -12$$
	$$x = \frac{3}{4}\cdot -12 = \boxed{-9}$$
	Since -9 is the only solution listed in the answer choices, answer choice A is correct.
9 D	$$Set\ A: \{3,4,5,5,5,5,6,7\}$$
	The mode is the number that appears in the set the most number of times. This means the mode is equal to 5.
	The median is the number in the center of the data. Since there are an even number of elements in the set, the median is the number in between the 4th and 5th elements of the set, which in this case is equal to 5.
	The mean is equal to the sum of all the elements in the set divided by the number of elements in the set. This is equal to $\frac{3+4+5+5+5+5+6+7}{8} = \frac{40}{8} = 5$
	The sum of the mode, median, and mean is equal to $5+5+5 = 15$
10 D	The 7 digit phone number can be represented visually as:
	$$5\ \_\ \_\ \_\ \_\ \_\ 3$$
	For the five blanks in the middle of the number, there are ten possibilities (0-9). This means that the total number of possible phone numbers is $10\cdot 10\cdot 10\cdot 10\cdot 10 = 100{,}000$.

11 B	The probability that a person is born with blue eyes is equal to 2%. This means that out of 100 people born in the hospital, 2 of them have blue eyes. For 150 people born in the hospital, $150 \cdot 0.02 = 3$ people have blue eyes.
12 D	$$-223 \leq 15x + 2 < 152$$ $$-225 \leq 15x < 150$$ $$-15 \leq x < 10$$ This means that the values of x can be equal to -15, but cannot be equal to 10.
13 D	The notation $(f + g)(x)$ shows the sum of the two functions $f(x)$ and $g(x)$. This sum is $x^2 + 2 + 2x - 2 = x^2 + 2x$.
14 D	Squaring both sides of the equation gives: $$3x + 1 = 2x$$ $$x = -1$$ If $x = -1$ is plugged back into the equation to check for a solution: $$\sqrt{3(-1) + 1} = \sqrt{2(-1)}$$ $$\sqrt{-2} = \sqrt{-2}$$ Recall that we cannot have a negative number inside the square root function, as it is undefined. This means that there is no solution. Additionally the graph below shows that the two functions never intersect, meaning that there is no solution. 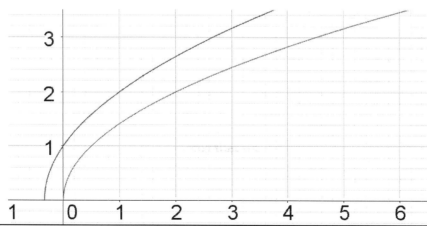
15 B	The average high temperature values shown are 70°C, 75°C, 80°C, and 85°C. Since the values are increasing at a constant rate of 5 degrees Celsius, the data is best described as a linear relationship.

| 16 B | Average speed = distance/time. The total distance that Tom traveled equals:

$$(7 \cdot 66) + (10 \cdot 85) = 1312 \; miles$$

The total time that Tom traveled was 17 hours, so:

$$\frac{1312 \; miles}{17 \; hours} = 77.2 \; miles \; per \; hour$$ |
|---|---|
| 17 A | Probability is the number of specific occurrences divided by the total number of occurences. The number of people who speak English as shown in the table is 141. The total number of participants is 216. The fractional probability is $\frac{141}{216}$. |
| 18 C | The total number of children aged 0-10 is 25. Out of these, 10 speak Spanish. This means that the overall probability is $\frac{10}{25} = \frac{2}{5}$. Expressed as a percentage, $\frac{2}{5}$ equals 40%. |
| 19 A | The coordinates from the word problem are:

$$(1,81), (2,27), (3,9)$$

Since the y-values are decreasing by 1/3 of the original value, this function is exponentially decaying. The best way to figure out the answer is to plug in any of these points into the answer choices. Plugging in the point $(1,81)$ into the answer choices gives:

Answer choice A: $h = 81 \left(\frac{1}{3}\right)^0 = 81$ Correct

Answer choice B : $h = 81 \cdot \left(\frac{1}{3}\right)^1 = 27$ Incorrect

Answer choice C: $h = \left(\frac{1}{3}\right)^1 = \frac{1}{3}$ Incorrect

Answer choice D: $h = \left(\frac{1}{3}\right) \cdot 1 = \frac{1}{3}$ Incorrect |
| 20 C | The sum of a and c must be greater than 50, non-inclusive. This can be represented as:

$$a + c > 50$$

The sum of 3a and 2c must be greater than or equal to 400. This can be represented as

$$a + 2c \geq 400$$ |
| 21 A | $$x = \frac{\sqrt{17} - 3}{\sqrt{2}}$$

Plugging this expression directly into a graphing calculator and rounding gives 0.79. |

22 80	Since the velocity increases at 2 meters per second every second for 60 seconds, the speed after these 60 seconds is $2 \cdot 60 = 120$ $meters\ per\ second$. While slowing down, the velocity decreases by $4 \cdot 10 = 40$ $meters\ per\ second$. This means the final velocity is $120 - 40 = 80$ $meters\ per\ second$.
23 10	The expansion of the expression using the FOIL method is: $$(2x + 1)(2x + 2) = 4x^2 + 4x + 2x + 2$$ $$4x^2 + 6x + 2$$ The coefficients of the variables are 4 and 6, and $4 + 6 = 10$
24 1341	In five years, Bank A has a total of : $$1000 \cdot 1.03 \cdot 1.03 \cdot 1.03 \cdot 1.03 \cdot 1.03 = 1159.27$$ In five years, Bank B has a total of: $$1000 + 300 + 300 + 300 + 300 + 300 = 2500$$ The difference between these two amounts is $2500 - 1159.27 = 1340.73$, which rounds to $1341
25 106	To have comparable ratios, the ratios given in the problem need to be multiplied by a number. To compare the green marbles between ratios, the first ratio must be multiplied by a factor of 2: $$2\ blue: 6\ green :: 6\ green: 3\ red$$ Now to compare the red marbles between the two ratios involving red, we must multiply the ratios above by a factor of 9: $$18\ blue: 54\ green :: 54\ green: 27\ red :: 27 red : 7\ black$$ Now that we have converted 3 separate ratios into one large ratio, the answer to the question is equal to $18\ blue + 54\ green + 27\ red + 7\ black = 106\ marbles$

Questions 1-8 are based on the following passage.

Passage 1

Read the following excerpt from Siddhartha, by Herman Hesse, and answer the questions that follow.

(1)   In the shade of the house, in the sunshine of the riverbank near the boats, in the shade of the Sal-wood forest, in the shade of the fig tree is where Siddhartha grew up, the

(5) handsome son of the Brahman, the young falcon, together with his friend Govinda, son of a Brahman. The sun tanned his light shoulders by the banks of the river when bathing, performing the sacred ablutions, the sacred

(10) offerings.   In the mango grove, shade poured into his black eyes, when playing as a boy, when his mother sang, when the sacred offerings were made, when his father, the scholar, taught him, when the wise men talked. For a long time,

(15) Siddhartha had been partaking in the discussions of the wise men, practicing debate with Govinda, practicing with Govinda the art of reflection, the service of meditation. He already knew how to speak the Om silently, the word of

(20) words, to speak it silently into himself while inhaling, to speak it silently out of himself while exhaling, with all the concentration of his soul, the forehead surrounded by the glow of the clear-thinking spirit. He already knew to feel

(25) Atman in the depths of his being, indestructible, one with the universe.

     Joy leapt in his father's heart for his son who was quick to learn, thirsty for knowledge; he saw him growing up to become great wise

(30) man and priest, a prince among the Brahmans. Bliss leapt in his mother's breast when she saw him, when she saw him walking, when she saw him sit down and get up, Siddhartha, strong, handsome, he who was walking on slender legs,

(35) greeting her with perfect respect.

     Love touched the hearts of the Brahmans' young daughters when Siddhartha walked through the lanes of the town with the luminous forehead, with the eye of a king, with

(40) his slim hips.

     But more than all the others he was loved by Govinda, his friend, the son of a Brahman. He loved Siddhartha's eye and sweet voice, he loved his walk and the perfect decency

(45) of his movements, he loved everything Siddhartha did and said and what he loved most was his spirit, his transcendent, fiery thoughts, his ardent will, his high calling. Govinda knew: he would not become a common Brahman, not

(55) a lazy official in charge of offerings; not a greedy merchant with magic spells; not a vain, vacuous speaker; not a mean, deceitful priest; and also not a decent, stupid sheep in the herd of the many. No, and he, Govinda, as well did

(60) not want to become one of those, not one of those tens of thousands of Brahmans. He wanted to follow Siddhartha, the beloved, the splendid. And in days to come, when Siddhartha would become a god, when he would join the

(65) glorious, then Govinda wanted to follow him as his friend, his companion, his servant, his spear-carrier, his shadow.

     Siddhartha was thus loved by everyone. He was a source of joy for everybody; he was a

(70) delight for them all.

     But he, Siddhartha, was not a source of joy for himself; he found no delight in himself. Walking the rosy paths of the fig tree garden, sitting in the bluish shade of the grove of

(75) contemplation, washing his limbs daily in the bath of repentance, sacrificing in the dim shade of the mango forest, his gestures of perfect decency, everyone's love and joy, he still lacked all joy in his heart. Dreams and restless

(80) thoughts came into his mind, flowing from the water of the river, sparkling from the stars of

the night, melting from the beams of the sun, dreams came to him and a restlessness of the soul, fuming from the sacrifices, breathing forth (85) from the verses of the Rig-Veda, being infused into him, drop by drop, from the teachings of the old Brahmans.

1. In lines 10-14 ("In...talked"), the author uses which of the following strategies?

A) Simile
B) Parallel structure
C) Onomatopoeia
D) Foreshadowing

2. The word "partaking" in line 15 most nearly means:

A) Participating
B) Praying
C) Promoting
D) Presuming

3. Which of the following best describes the personality of Siddhartha?

A) Siddhartha is a rude child who does not listen to his elders
B) Siddhartha does not believe in his religion and is forced to study it
C) Siddhartha is a pious child with a deep connection to his religion
D) Siddhartha is not worthy enough to study his religion

4. Which choice most effectively supports the answer to the previous question?

A) Lines 14-16 ("For...men")
B) Lines 18-24 ("He already...spirit")
C) Line 26-27 ("Joy...knowledge")
D) Line 31-35 ("Bliss...respect")

5. Lines 27-35 describe Siddhartha as

A) An intelligent yet arrogant child
B) An ideal son and future king of his land
C) A diseased and feeble child without a future
D) A depressed and angry priest who depends on his parents

6. The word "luminous" in line 39 most nearly means:

A) Glowing
B) Sweaty
C) Intriguing
D) Inexplicable

7. Which of the following best describes the shift in the narrator's attitude from line 70 to line 71?

A) Angry to Accusatory
B) Fear to Uninterested
C) Positive to Conflicting
D) Bored to Confident

8. Which of the following best describes the main idea of this passage?

A) Siddhartha was a valiant child prince who followed his elders and their religion, but did not enjoy his life and feared for his future
B) Siddhartha was a model child who had all of his whims and demands answered by his father, the king
C) Siddhartha used his superiority to belittle other children and assert his dominance
D) Siddhartha was brought up by his parents who decided that he would not be fit to be the next king due to his lack of faith

Questions 9-16 are based on the following passage.

Passage 2

Read the following excerpt on the effects of World War 1 and answer the questions that follow.

(1)   World War I was one of the most destructive wars in modern history. Nearly ten million soldiers died as a result of hostilities. The enormous losses on all sides of the conflict
(5) resulted in part from the introduction of new weapons, like the machine gun and gas warfare, as well as the failure of military leaders to adjust their tactics to the increasingly mechanized nature of warfare. A policy of
(10) attrition, particularly on the Western Front, cost the lives of hundreds of thousands of soldiers.

No official agencies kept careful accounting of civilian losses during the war years, but scholars suggest that as many as
(15) thirteen million non-combatants died as a direct or indirect result of the war. The conflict uprooted or displaced millions of persons from their homes in Europe and Asia Minor. Property and industry losses were catastrophic,
(20) especially in France, Belgium, Poland, and Serbia, where fighting had been heaviest.

In January 1918, some ten months before the end of World War I, US President Woodrow Wilson had written a list of proposed
(25) war aims which he called the "Fourteen Points." Eight of these points dealt specifically with territorial and political settlements associated with the victory of the Entente Powers, including the idea of national self-
(30) determination for ethnic populations in Europe. The remainder of the principles focused on preventing war in the future, the last proposing a League of Nations to arbitrate international disputes. Wilson hoped his proposal would
(35) bring about a just and lasting peace, a "peace without victory."

When German leaders signed the armistice in the Compiègne Forest on 11 November, 1918, many of them believed that
(40) the Fourteen Points would form the basis of the future peace treaty, but when the heads of the governments of the United States, Great Britain, France, and Italy met in Paris to discuss treaty terms, the European contingent of the
(45) "Big Four" rejected this approach.

Viewing Germany as the chief instigator of the conflict, the European Allied Powers decided to impose particularly stringent treaty obligations upon the defeated Germany. The
(50) Treaty of Versailles, presented for German leaders to sign on May 7, 1919, forced Germany to concede territories to Belgium (Eupen-Malmédy), Czechoslovakia (the Hultschin district), and Poland (Poznan [German: Posen],
(55) West Prussia and Upper Silesia). The Germans returned Alsace and Lorraine, annexed in 1871 after the Franco-Prussian War, to France. All German overseas colonies became League of

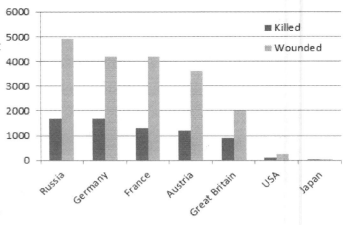

Casualties By Country (in thousands)

Nation Mandates, and the city of Danzig (today:
(60) Gdansk), with its large ethnically German population, became a Free City. The treaty demanded demilitarization and occupation of the Rhineland, and special status for the Saarland under French control. Plebiscites were
(65) to determine the future of areas in northern Schleswig on the Danish-German frontier and parts of Upper Silesia on the border with Poland.

Perhaps the most humiliating portion of
(70) the treaty for defeated Germany was Article

231, commonly known as the "War Guilt Clause," which forced the German nation to accept complete responsibility for initiating World War I. As such Germany was liable for all
(75) material damages, and France's premier Georges Clemenceau particularly insisted on imposing enormous reparation payments. Aware that Germany would probably not be able to pay such a towering debt, Clemenceau
(80) and the French nevertheless greatly feared rapid German recovery and the initiation of a new war against France. Hence, the French sought in the postwar treaty to limit Germany's potential to regain its economic superiority and
(85) to rearm. The German army was to be limited to 100,000 men, and conscription proscribed; the treaty restricted the Navy to vessels under 10,000 tons, with a ban on the acquisition or maintenance of a submarine fleet.

9. The author places the blame for the death of millions of soldiers on:

A) American involvement in the European theater
B) Unrestricted submarine warfare
C) Adolf Hitler's regime
D) Poor military leadership

10. Based on the information found in lines 22-36, President Woodrow Wilson can best be described as:

A) Unable to make useful political decisions
B) Fearful of communism
C) Able to make compromises
D) Against American involvement in foreign affairs

11. The word "stringent" in line 48 most nearly means:

A) Interesting
B) Harsh
C) Rope-like
D) Regulations

12. The information found in the graphic above supports which point made in the passage?

A) The high amount of Russian casualties allowed for the Americans to punish Germany further
B) The high amount of German casualties was due to the fact that Germany started the war
C) The lower amount of American casualties allowed for Americans to declare victory in WWI
D) The lower amount of Japanese casualties allowed for Japan to join the Axis powers in WWII

13. The passage implies that the German territory losses:

A) Caused Germany to lose a large amount of territory that was gained from past conflicts
B) Did not have any effect on Germany as a country
C) Caused the conflicts in World War II
D) Allowed Germany to refocus on their economy at home

14. Which of the following is a reason for the creation of the War Guilt Clause in the Treaty of Versailles?

A) To convince Germans to join the Allied powers in exchange for war debt relief
B) To increase the wealth of the Allied powers
C) To make fun of the losing side of the World War
D) To avoid a future conflict by hindering Germany's ability to progress

15. Which choice most effectively supports the answer to the previous question?

A) Lines 69-71 ("Perhaps...Article 231")
B) Lines 74-77 ("As...payments")
C) Lines 78-82 ("Aware...France")
D) Lines 85-89 ("The German...fleet")

16. The word "restricted" in line 87 most nearly means:

A) Possessed
B) Acquired
C) Limited
D) Caused

Questions 17-25 are based on the following passage.

Passage 3

Read the following article from ScienceNews regarding the recent Zika virus outbreak and answer the questions that follow.

(1)   The Zika virus probably arrived in the Western Hemisphere from somewhere in the Pacific more than a year before it was detected, a new genetic analysis of the epidemic shows.
(5) Researchers also found that as Zika fanned outward from Brazil, it entered neighboring countries and South Florida multiple times without being noticed.
      Although Zika quietly took root in
(10)northeastern Brazil in late 2013 or early 2014, many months passed before Brazilian health authorities received reports of unexplained fever and skin rashes. Zika was finally confirmed as the culprit in April 2015.
(15)   The World Health Organization did not declare the epidemic a public health emergency until February 2016, after babies of Zika-infected mothers began to be born with severe neurological problems. Zika, which is carried by
(20)mosquitoes, infected an estimated 1 million people in Brazil alone in 2015, and is now thought to be transmitted in 84 countries worldwide.
      Although Zika's path was documented
(25)starting in 2015 through records of human cases, less was known about how the virus spread so silently before detection, or how outbreaks in different parts of Central and South America were connected. Now two
(30)groups working independently, reporting online May 24 in *Nature*, have compared samples from different times and locations to read the history recorded in random mutations of the virus's 10 genes.
(35)   One team, led by scientists in the United Kingdom and Brazil, drove more than 1,200 miles across Brazil— "a *Top Gear*–style road trip," one scientist quipped — with a portable device that could produce a complete

(40) catalog of the virus's genes in less than a day. A second team, led by researchers at the Broad Institute of MIT and Harvard, analyzed more than 100 Zika genomes from infected patients and mosquitoes in nine countries and Puerto

(45) Rico. Based on where the cases originated, and the estimated rate at which genetic changes appear, the scientists re-created Zika's evolutionary timeline.

Together, the studies revealed an

(50) epidemic that was silently churning long before anyone knew. "We found that in each of the regions we could analyze, Zika virus circulated undetected for many months, up to a year or longer, before the first locally transmitted cases

(55) were reported," says Bronwyn MacInnis, an infectious disease geneticist at the Broad Institute, in Cambridge, Mass. "This means the outbreak in these regions was under way much earlier than previously thought."

(60) Although the epidemic exploded out of Brazil, the scientists also found a remote possibility of early settlement in the Caribbean. "It's not immediately clear whether Zika stopped off somewhere else in the Americas

(65) before it got to northeast Brazil," said Oliver Pybus, who studies evolution and infectious disease at the University of Oxford in England.

In a third study reported in *Nature*, researchers from 30 different institutions

(70) followed a trail of genetic clues to determine when and how Zika made its way to Florida. Those researchers concluded that Zika was introduced multiple times into the Miami area, most likely from the Caribbean, before

(75) local mosquitoes picked it up. The number of human cases increased in step with the rise in

mosquito populations, said Kristian Andersen, an infectious disease researcher at the Scripps Research Institute in La Jolla, Calif. "Focusing on

(80) getting rid of mosquitoes is an effective way of preventing human cases," he says.

17. Lines 1-4 ("The...shows") from the passage imply that:

A) The Zika virus originated from the Saharan desert
B) The origin of the Zika virus was unknown to scientists until the disease was analyzed
C) The Zika virus is a complete mystery to scientists throughout the world
D) The Western Hemisphere allowed the Zika virus to generate in breeding mosquito populations

18. The word "culprit" in line 14 most nearly means:

A) Robber
B) Guardian
C) Negotiator
D) Perpetrator

19. Which of the following was the reason for the declaration of the Zika virus as a public health emergency?

A) It began infecting millions of people in Brazil alone
B) Scientists were unable to find a cure for the virus, resulting in a state of worldwide panic
C) Mosquitoes began spreading the virus through pathogens in the air, causing millions to become infected
D) Many children were born with severe brain damage, resulting in a state of panic

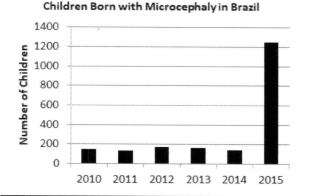

Children Born with Microcephaly in Brazil

20. Which choice most effectively supports the answer to the previous question?
A) Lines 15-19 ("The...problems")
B) Lines 24-27 ("Although...detection")
C) Lines 29-34 ("Now...genes")
D) Lines 35-37 ("One...Brazil")

21. Which of the following is a difference in the Zika virus study methods of group 1 and group 2?

A) Study group 1 focused on the genetics of the Zika virus whereas study group 2 studied how the disease evolved
B) Study group 1 worked in the US, whereas study group 2 worked in Brazil
C) Study group 1 was unable to generate results, whereas study group 2 was able to find the cure for the Zika virus
D) Study group 1 used the results of study group 2 to synthesize a cure for the Zika virus.

22. The word "undetected" in line 53 most nearly means:

A) Exposed
B) Secretive
C) Detached
D) Interrupted

23. Which of the following best describes the attitude of Professor Oliver Pybus as found in Lines 63-67?

A) Condescending
B) Depressed
C) Angry
D) Uncertain

24. The graph included in the passage best supports information found in which of the following lines?

A) Lines 68-72 ("In...Florida)
B) Lines 72-74 ("Those...Caribbean")
C) Lines 75-77 ("The...populations")
D) Lines 78-79 ("an infectious...Calif.")

25. Which of the following is a solution for the Zika issue as stated in the passage?

A) Changing the location of the 2016 Olympics to prevent the virus from spreading internationally
B) Setting cities infected with the Zika virus on fire
C) Destroying mosquito populations
D) Finding a cure immediately for the Zika virus

Questions 26-34 are based on the following excerpts.

Passage 4

Excerpt 1

Read the following excerpt from an anti-World War 1 essay written by Randolph Bourne.

(1)　　　To those of us who still retain an irreconcilable animus against war, it has been a bitter experience to see the unanimity with which the American intellectuals have thrown
(5)　their support to the use of war-technique in the crisis in which America found herself. Socialists, college professors, publicists, new-republicans, practitioners of literature, have vied with each other in confirming with their intellectual faith
(10)　the collapse of neutrality and the riveting of the war-mind on a hundred million more of the world's people. And the intellectuals are not content with confirming our belligerent gesture. They are now complacently asserting that it was
(15)　they who effectively willed it, against the hesitation and dim perceptions of the American democratic masses. A war made deliberately by the intellectuals!
　　　Those intellectuals who have felt
(20)　themselves totally out of sympathy with this drag toward war will seek some explanation for this joyful leadership. They will want to understand this willingness of the American intellect to open the sluices and flood us with
(25)　the sewage of the war spirit. We cannot forget the virtuous horror and stupefaction which filled our college professors when they read the famous manifesto of their ninety-three German colleagues in defense of their war. To the
(30)　American academic mind of 1914 defense of war was inconceivable. . . . They would have thought anyone mad who talked of shipping American men by the hundreds of thousands— conscripts—to die on the fields of France. Such
(35)　a spiritual change seems catastrophic when we shoot our minds back to those days when neutrality was a proud thing. But the intellectual progress has been so gradual that the country retains little sense of the irony. The
(40)　war sentiment, begun so gradually but so perseveringly by the preparedness advocates who came from the ranks of big business, caught hold of one after another of the intellectual groups.

Excerpt 2

Read the following excerpt from a Woodrow Wilson pro-World War 1 speech and answer the questions that follow

(45)　　　I have called the Congress into extraordinary session because there are serious, very serious, choices of policy to be made, and made immediately, which it was neither right nor constitutionally permissible
(50)　that I should assume the responsibility of making. On the 3rd of February, I officially laid before you the extraordinary announcement of the Imperial German government that on and after the 1st day of February it was its purpose
(55)　to put aside all restraints of law or of humanity and use its submarines to sink every vessel that sought to approach either the ports of Great Britain and Ireland or the western coasts of Europe or any of the ports controlled by the
(60)　enemies of Germany within the Mediterranean.
　　　That had seemed to be the object of the German submarine warfare earlier in the war, but since April of last year the Imperial government had somewhat restrained the
(65)　commanders of its undersea craft in conformity with its promise then given to us that passenger boats should not be sunk and that due warning would be given to all other vessels which its submarines might seek to destroy, when no
(70)　resistance was offered or escape attempted, and care taken that their crews were given at least a fair chance to save their lives in their open boats. The precautions taken were meager and haphazard enough, as was proved
(75)　in distressing instance after instance in the progress of the cruel and unmanly business, but a certain degree of restraint was observed.
　　　The new policy has swept every restriction aside. Vessels of every kind,

(80) whatever their flag, their character, their cargo, their destination, their errand, have been ruthlessly sent to the bottom without warning and without thought of help or mercy for those on board, the vessels of friendly neutrals along
(85) with those of belligerents. Even hospital ships and ships carrying relief to the sorely bereaved and stricken people of Belgium, though the latter were provided with safe conduct through the proscribed areas by the German
(90) government itself and were distinguished by unmistakable marks of identity, have been sunk with the same reckless lack of compassion or of principle.

26. The author of the first excerpt can best be described as:

A) An opponent of capitalism
B) A social critic
C) A soldier fearful of war
D) The president of the United States

27. In the first excerpt, the speaker accuses the people of the United States of

A) having a limited intellect and making a bad decision in sending millions of soldiers overseas
B) dropping the atomic bomb on Japan without thinking of the casualties
C) destroying the US economy by shipping men overseas
D) creating an economic bubble that would lead to the stock market crash

28. The word "sentiment" in line 40 most nearly means:

A) Attitude
B) Learning
C) Romanticism
D) Persuasion

29. Lines 45-51 ("I have...making") imply that Woodrow Wilson

A) Is too afraid to instigate a war with Germany
B) Is too lazy and asks Congress to solve his problems for him
C) Does not have the authority to declare war on Germany
D) Is interested in partnering with Germany to reach a peace treaty

30. Wilson describes the attack on civilian ships by German submarines as

A) Fearful
B) Brash
C) Wise
D) Responsible

31. The purpose of excerpt 2 is

A) To catalog the types of ships that were sunk by the Germans
B) To describe the horrors of unrestricted submarine warfare to the American public
C) To persuade Congress to declare war on the Germans
D) To ridicule the American government for not allowing the president to solely declare war

32. Which choice best states the relationship between the two excerpts?

A) Excerpt 1 opposes the argument presented in Excerpt 2
B) Excerpt 1 supports the argument presented in Excerpt 2
C) Excerpt 2 provides evidence for the argument presented in Excerpt 1
D) Excerpt 1 provides evidence for the argument presented in Excerpt 2

33. A difference between the two excerpts is that

A) Excerpt 1 addresses the American public, whereas Excerpt 2 addresses Congress only
B) Excerpt 2 uses an extended metaphor, whereas Excerpt 1 does not use any symbolic language at all
C) Excerpt 1 addresses the lower class Americans, whereas Excerpt 2 addresses higher class Americans
D) Excerpt 1 addresses the President, whereas Excerpt 2 addresses society as a whole

34. How would Wilson most likely respond to Bourne's statement in lines 31-34 ("They...France")?

A) He would work with Bourne to come up with a negotiation treaty with Germany
B) He would accept that sending troops overseas is unnecessary
C) He would agree with Bourne's statement
D) He would point out that the reason the Americans entered the war was to save more civilian lives

Questions 35-42 are based on the following excerpts

Passage 5

Read the following excerpt from ScienceNews on facial feature encoding and then answer the questions that follow.

(1)   A monkey's brain builds a picture of a human face somewhat like a Mr. Potato Head — piecing it together bit by bit.
    The code that a monkey's brain uses to
(5) represent faces relies not on groups of nerve cells tuned to specific faces — as has been previously proposed — but on a population of about 200 cells that code for different sets of facial characteristics. Added together, the
(10) information contributed by each nerve cell lets the brain efficiently capture any face, researchers reported.
    "It's a turning point in neuroscience — a major breakthrough," says Rodrigo Quian
(15) Quiroga, a neuroscientist at the University of Leicester in England who wasn't part of the work. "It's a very simple mechanism to explain something as complex as recognizing faces."
    Until now, Quiroga says, the leading
(20) explanation for the way the primate brain recognizes faces proposed that individual nerve cells, or neurons, respond to certain types of faces. A system like that might work for the few dozen people with whom you regularly interact.
(25) But accounting for all of the peripheral people encountered in a lifetime would require a lot of neurons.
    It now seems that the brain might have a more efficient strategy, says Doris Tsao, a
(30) neuroscientist at Caltech.
    Tsao and coauthor Le Chang used statistical analyses to identify 50 variables that accounted for the greatest differences between 200 face photos. Those variables represented
(35) somewhat complex changes in the face — for instance, the hairline rising while the face becomes wider and the eyes become further-set.

The researchers turned those variables (40) into a 50-dimensional "face space," with each face being a point and each dimension being an axis along which a set of features varied.

Then, Tsao and Chang extracted 2,000 faces from that map, each linked to specific (45) coordinates. While projecting the faces one at a time onto screens in front of two macaque monkeys, the team recorded the activity in single neurons in parts of the monkey's temporal lobe known to respond specifically to (50) faces. Altogether, the recordings captured activity from 205 neurons.

Each face cell was tuned to one of the 50 axes previously identified, Tsao and Chang found. The rate at which each cell sent electrical (55) signals was proportional to a given face's coordinate position along an axis. But a cell didn't respond to changes in features not captured by that axis. For instance, a cell tuned to an axis where nose width and eye size (60) changed wouldn't respond to changes in lip shape.

Adding together the features conveyed by each cell's activity creates a picture of a complete face. And like a computer creating a (65) full-color display by mixing different proportions of red, green and blue light, the coordinate system lets a brain paint any face in a spectrum.

"It was a total surprise," Tsao says. Even (70) when the faces were turned in profile, the same cells still responded to the same features.

Tsao and Chang were then able to re-create that process in reverse using an algorithm. When they plugged in the activity (75) patterns of the 205 recorded neurons, the computer spat out an image that looked almost exactly like what they had shown the monkeys.

"People view neurons as black boxes," says Ed Connor, a neuroscientist at Johns (80) Hopkins University who wasn't part of the study. "This is a striking demonstration that you can really understand what the brain is doing."

Elsewhere in the brain, though, neurons don't use this facial coordinate system. In 2005, (85) Quiroga discovered individual neurons attuned to particular people in the hippocampus, a part of the brain involved in memory. He found, for instance, a single neuron that fired off messages in response to a photo of Jennifer (90) Aniston or conceptually related images, like her name written out or a picture of her Friends costar Lisa Kudrow.

The new results fit well into that picture, Tsao and Quiroga agree. Tsao compares (95) her system to a GPS for facial identity. "These cells are coding the coordinates. And you can use these coordinates for anything you want. You can build a specific lookup table that codes these into specific identities — like Barack (100) Obama, or your mother."

Quiroga's hippocampal cells, just a few neural connections away, are like the output of that table — a sort of speed dial for people and concepts previously encountered.

(105) The different coding strategies might be tied to differences in what these brain areas do. "When we remember things, we forget details but we remember concepts," Quiroga says. But for telling faces apart, and especially for (110) processing unfamiliar faces, "details are key."

35. Lines 1-2 ("A...Head") use which of the following techniques?

A) Parallel Structure
B) Appeal to Emotion
C) Onomatopoeia
D) Simile

36. Which of the following describes how a monkey recognizes a face?

A) The monkey uses a specialized group of cells to differentiate facial features
B) The monkey uses a group of nerve cells in the brain to identify different faces
C) The monkey uses a camera-like mechanism in its eye to capture facial features
D) The monkey has a special thermal imaging system to differentiate facial features

37. The word "leading" in line 19 most nearly means:

A) Edging
B) Primary
C) First
D) Interesting

38. The hyphen used in line 35 primarily serves to:

A) Provide an interesting piece of information unrelated to the passage
B) Provide a definition for an uncommon word
C) Serve as a placeholder for missing information
D) Explain one example of a variable in the study

39. The information found in lines 69-71 ("It...features") most likely indicates that

A) The information from Tsao and Chang's study was not useful at all
B) The information found in the study by Tsao and Chang provided unanticipated results
C) The information from Tsao and Chang's study was expected
D) Tsao and Chang were unable to extract useful information from the primates

40. What is the intended effect of including names of famous celebrities in lines 87-92 and lines 99-100?

A) To prove that science can connect with other aspects of humanity
B) To add a sense of humor to the article
C) To show that the author enjoys the works of these celebrities
D) To give examples of people with distinct facial features

41. The word "concepts" in line 108 most nearly means:

A) Ideas
B) Facts
C) Hypotheses
D) Constructs

42. The primary purpose of this passage is to

A) Persuade the reader to donate to fund new research on primates
B) Inform the reader about a new discovery in the way the brain functions
C) Entertain the reader with an interesting story on primates
D) Inform the reader that the primates are endangered and in risk of extinction

Questions 1-10 are based on the following passage.

Before you discuss the resolution, let me place before you one or two [1] things I want you to understand two things very clearly and to consider them from the same point of view from which I am placing them before you. I ask you to consider it from my point of view, because if you approve of it, you will be enjoined to carry out all I say. It will be a great responsibility. There are people who ask me whether I am the same man that I was in 1920, or whether there has been any change in me. You are right in asking that question.

Let me, however, hasten to assure that I am the same Gandhi as I was in 1920. [2] If at all, my emphasis on it has grown stronger. There is no real contradiction between the present resolution and my previous writings and utterances.

Occasions like the present do not occur in everybody's and but rarely in anybody's life. I want you to know and feel that there is nothing but purest Ahimsa in all that I am [3] saying, reciting, and speaking today. The draft resolution of the Working Committee is based on Ahimsa, the contemplated struggle similarly has its roots in Ahimsa. If, therefore, there is any among you who has lost faith in Ahimsa or is wearied of it, let him not vote for this resolution.

1.
A) NO CHANGE
B) things, I
C) things: I
D) things = I

2. At this point the writer is considering adding the following sentence:

I attach the same importance to nonviolence that I did then.

Should the writer make this addition here?

A) Yes, because this shows why he is the same as the Gandhi from 1920
B) Yes, because this is a humorous statement for the audience
C) No, because it is irrelevant to the main idea of the passage
D) No, because Gandhi has dramatically changed since 1920

3.
A) NO CHANGE
B) saying, and reciting, and speaking
C) saying and speaking
D) saying

Let me explain my position clearly. God has vouchsafed to me a priceless gift in the weapon of Ahimsa. [4] I and my Ahimsa are on our trail today. If in the present crisis, when the earth is being scorched by the flames of Him and crying for deliverance, I failed to make use of the God given talent, God will not forgive me and I shall be judged unwrongly of the great gift. I must act now. I may not hesitate and merely look on, when Russia and China are threatened.

Ours is not a drive for power, but purely a nonviolent fight for India's independence [5] without fighting. In a violent struggle, a successful general has been often known to cause a military coup and to set up a [6] dictatorship. But under the Congress scheme of things, essentially nonviolent as it is, there can be no room for dictatorship. A non-violent soldier of freedom will covet nothing for himself; he fights only for the freedom of his country. The Congress is unconcerned as to who will rule, when freedom is attained.

The power [7] when it comes will belong to the people of India, and it will be for them to decide to whom it placed in the entrusted. May be that the reins will be placed in the hands of the Parsis, for instance-as I would love to see happen-or they may be handed to some others whose names are not heard in the Congress today. It will not be for you

4.
A) NO CHANGE
B) Me and my Ahimsa
C) I my and Ahimsa
D) My Ahimsa and I

5. Which of the following revisions improves the flow of the sentence?

A) NO CHANGE
B) intensely fighting
C) fighting hard
D) Remove the underlined phrase

6.
A) NO CHANGE
B) dictatorship. And
C) dictatorship; but
D) dictatorship, but

7.
A) NO CHANGE
B) :when it comes:
C) -when it comes
D) , when it comes,

then to object saying, "This community is microscopic. That party did not play its due part in the freedom's struggle; why should it have all the power?" Ever since [8] its inception the Congress has kept itself meticulously free of the communal taint. It has thought always in terms of the whole nation and has acted accordingly... I know how imperfect our Ahimsa is and how far away we are still from the ideal, but in Ahimsa there is no final failure or defeat. I have faith, therefore, that if, in spite of our shortcomings, the big thing does happen, it will be because God wanted to help us by crowning with success our silent, unremitting Sadhana for the last [9] twenty two years.

[1] Everybody will be their own master. [2] I believe that in the history of the world, there has not been a more genuinely democratic struggle for freedom than ours. [3] I read Carlyle's French Resolution while I was in prison, and Pandit Jawaharlal has told me something about the Russian revolution. [5] But it is my conviction that inasmuch as these struggles were fought with the weapon of violence they failed to realize the democratic ideal. [5] In the democracy which I have envisaged, a democracy established by nonviolence, there will be equal freedom for all. [6] It is to join a struggle for such democracy that I invite you today. [7] Once you realize this you will forget the differences between the Hindus and Muslims, and think of yourselves as Indians only, engaged in the common struggle for independence. [10]

8.
A) NO CHANGE
B) its's
C) it's
D) it is

9.
A) NO CHANGE
B) twenty: two
C) twenty-two
D) twentietwo

10. For the sake of cohesion, sentence 1 should be placed :

A) NO CHANGE
B) after sentence 2
C) after sentence 5
D) after sentence 7

Questions 11-20 are based on the following passage.

[1]

When you sit down for breakfast, [11] your probably not thinking about every step in the supply chain that ultimately allowed you to pour a bowl of cereal. However, for scientists and policymakers, understanding this complicated process is an important step toward ensuring food security in the United States and across the globe.

[2]

NASA satellites are constantly keeping a close eye on our planet. And their observations are helping farmers, scientists, and policymakers develop strategies to improve food production and availability. [12]

[3]

One major factor that influences food security is the availability of water. When an area has plenty of water, crops [13] thrive, grow, and live, and livestock have plenty of lush grass to graze on. However, even just a few dry months can have a dramatic impact on a region's food production.

[4]

Several NASA missions are closely monitoring the water on our planet. [14] These satellites collect information about soil moisture, flooding and drought, groundwater and crop health.

11.
A) NO CHANGE
B) you'r
C) your's
D) you're

12. The author wishes to add a piece of information at this point in the passage. Based on the graph provided at the end of the passage, which of the following would be the most relevant addition?

A) Global warming has affected world in a negative way in the past 50 years
B) Thanks to these observations, a sufficient food supply has been generated for the increasing population
C) The population grows faster than the food supply
D) Mass famines will become more frequent in the future due to poor observations by scientists

13.
A) NO CHANGE
B) thrive and grow and live
C) thrive and grow
D) thrive

14. Which of the following is the best way to rewrite this sentence?

A) NO CHANGE
B) These satellites collect information about soil moisture, flooding, drought, groundwater and crop health
C) These satellites collect information about soil moisture, flooding, drought, groundwater, and crop health
D) These satellites collect information about soil moisture and, flooding and, drought, and groundwater, and crop health

[5]

One mission, called SMAP $\boxed{15}$, plays a particularly important role in understanding the impact of droughts. From orbit, SMAP measures the amount of water in the top 2 inches (5 centimeters) of soil everywhere on Earth. This top layer of soil is where we grow the food we eat.

[6]

The soil moisture data from SMAP is also sent to a USDA tool called Crop Explorer, which can be used by farmers and those who work in foreign agricultural policy. The tool can be used to see how severe the drought is in a specific area. It can also provide a prediction about approximately how long a drought might last.

[7]

SMAP is orbiting 426 miles (685 km) above, but it can see through layers of Earth's atmosphere and vegetation and into the soil using microwaves. These observations are used to make global maps of soil moisture and improve our understanding of how water and carbon circulate on Earth. $\boxed{16}$

[8]

If an area is in a severe drought that is expected to last for a while, information from the tool can help farmers decide if $\boxed{17}$ their need to change their crops or their planting practices. In this way, the tool can possibly help farmers to produce more food with less water.

15. At this point the writer is considering adding the following statement:

—short for Soil Moisture Active Passive—

Should the writer make this addition here?

A) Yes, because it clarifies an acronym previously stated
B) Yes, because it persuades the reader to actively pursue soil analysis
C) No, because it is irrelevant to the main idea of the passage
D) No, because it is not an interesting piece of information

16. For the sake of cohesion, paragraph 7 should be placed:

A) NO CHANGE
B) Before paragraph 2
C) Before paragraph 6
D) After paragraph 9

17.
A) NO CHANGE
B) their's
C) they're
D) they'll

[9]

Soil moisture data from SMAP can also be used by scientists to simulate future crop growth. These simulations could one day help farmers plan how they will harvest and manage specific crops [18] in the future.

[10]

For many people around the world, the oceans are also a rich source of food—from fish and shellfish to seaweed and algae. [19] Therefore, Earth's warming climate could mean drastic changes for these very sensitive ocean ecosystems. Several NASA missions are closely monitoring changes in the oceans—information that can also be used to help determine the health of ocean life.

[11]

NASA satellites collect information about ocean temperature and color, ocean currents, winds and severe storms, and melting sea ice. These measurements can help scientists better understand how quickly the oceans are changing. The data can also help scientists estimate the health of the oceans and how well they are supporting sea life—as well as the amount of seafood produced by the ocean.

[12]

For example, although the ocean may appear deep blue to the naked eye, there [20] is regions of the ocean that are actually slightly green. The color comes from chlorophyll—a green pigment found in

18.
A) NO CHANGE
B) futuristic
C) future
D) DELETE the underlined portion

19. The author wishes to change this transition word with one that indicates contrast. Which of the following is the best replacement?

A) NO CHANGE
B) Thereby
C) However
D) Interestingly

20.
A) NO CHANGE
B) were
C) have
D) are

tiny marine organisms called phytoplankton. Chlorophyll helps the phytoplankton turn sunlight and carbon dioxide into food and oxygen.

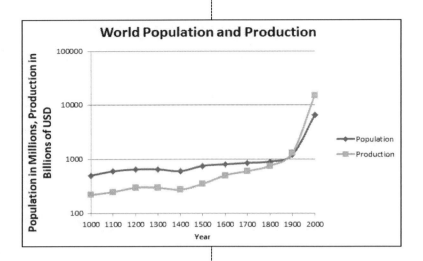

Questions 21-30 are based on the following passage.

When we consider the heroic resistance made by the French Army against heavy odds in this battle, the enormous losses inflicted upon the enemy and the evident exhaustion of the [21] enemy, it may well be the thought that these 25 divisions of the best-trained and best-equipped troops might have turned the scale. However, General Weygand had to fight without them. Only three British divisions or their equivalent were able to stand in the line with their French comrades. [22] They have suffered severely. They have fought well. We sent every man we could to France as fast as we could re-equip and transport their formations.

I am not reciting these facts for the purpose of recrimination. That I judge to be utterly futile and even harmful. We cannot afford it. I recite them in order to explain why it was we did not have, as we could have had, between twelve and fourteen British divisions fighting in the line in this great battle instead of only three. Now I put all this aside. I put it on the shelf, from which the historians, when they have time, will select their documents to tell their stories. We have to think of the future and not of the past. This also [23] applied in a small way to our own affairs at home. There are many who would hold an inquest in the House of Commons on

21.
A) NO CHANGE
B) enemy it may
C) enemy: it may
D) enemy; it may

22. Which of the following is the best revision combining these two sentences?

A) NO CHANGE
B) They have suffered severely, but they have fought well
C) They have suffered severely while they have fought well
D) They have suffered severely- and they have fought well

23.
A) NO CHANGE
B) applies
C) had applied
D) applying

the conduct of the Governments-and of Parliaments, for they are in it, too-during the years which led up to this catastrophe. They seek to indict those who were responsible for the guidance of our affairs. This also would be a foolish and pernicious process. There are too many in it. Let each man [24] migrate his conscience and search his speeches. I frequently search mine.

Of this I am quite sure, that if we open a quarrel between the past and the present, we shall find that we have lost the future. Therefore, I cannot accept the drawing of any distinctions between Members of the present Government. It was formed at a moment of crisis in order to unite all the Parties and all sections of opinion. It has received the almost unanimous support of both Houses of Parliament. [25] Its members are going to stand together, and, subject to the authority of the House of Commons, we are going to govern the country and fight the war.

It is absolutely necessary at a time like this that every Minister who tries each day to do his duty shall be respected; and their subordinates must know that their chiefs are not threatened men, men who are here today and gone tomorrow, but that their directions must be punctually and [26] truly obeyed. Without this concentrated power we cannot face what lies before us. I should not think it would be very advantageous for the House to prolong this Debate this afternoon under conditions

24. Which of the following choices could best replace the underlined word in order to make the sentence clearer?
A) NO CHANGE
B) lose
C) search
D) create

25.
A) NO CHANGE
B) it's
C) its's
D) it is

26.
A) NO CHANGE
B) faithfully
C) intricately
D) abusively

of public stress. Many facts are not clear that will be clear in a short time. We are to have a secret session on [27] Thursday and I should think that would be a better opportunity for the many earnest expressions of opinion which Members will desire to make and for the House to discuss vital matters without having everything read the next morning by our dangerous foes.

The disastrous military events which have happened during the past fortnight have not come to me with any sense of surprise. [28] Indeed, I indicated a fortnight ago as clearly as I could to the House that the worst possibilities were open. During the last few days we have successfully brought off the great majority of the troops we had on the line of communication in France; and seven-eighths of the troops we have sent to France since the beginning of the war [29] -that is to say, about 350,000 out of 400,000 men: are safely back in this country.

Others are still [30] fiting with the French, and fighting with considerable success in their local encounters against the enemy. We have also brought back a great mass of stores, rifles and munitions of all kinds which had been accumulated in France during the last nine months.

27.
A) NO CHANGE
B) Thursday-
C) Thursday:
D) Thursday,

28. At this point the writer is considering adding the following statement:

> As the leader of the British, I am never surprised by anything.

Should the writer make this addition here?

A) Yes, as it adds value to the paragraph by explaining the role of the speaker
B) Yes, because the statement is crucial to define the role of the British in the war
C) No, because the statement does not relate to the main idea of the passage
D) No, because the statement is not interesting for the audience to listen to

29.
A) NO CHANGE
B) -that is to say, about 350,000 out of 400,000 men-
C) :that is to say, about 350,000 out of 400,000 men:
D) "that is to say, about 350,000 out of 400,000 men"

30.
A) NO CHANGE
B) fitting
C) fiteing
D) fighting

Questions 31-40 are based on the following passage.

A new NASA, and Department of Energy, funded study finds that recent [31] increases in global methane levels observed since 2007 are not necessarily due to increasing emissions, but instead may be due to changes in how long methane remains in the atmosphere after it is emitted.

The second most important human-produced greenhouse gas after [32] carbon dioxide methane is colorless, odorless and can be hard to track. The gas has a wide range of [33] places, from decomposing biological material to leaks in natural gas pipelines. In the early 2000s, atmospheric scientists studying methane found that its global concentration — which had increased for decades, driven by methane emissions from fossil fuels and agriculture — leveled off as the sources of methane reached a balance with its destruction mechanisms. [34]

Previous studies of the renewed increase have focused on high-latitude wetlands or fossil fuels, Asian agricultural growth, or tropical wetlands as potential sources of the increased emissions. But in a study published today in the early online edition of the Proceedings of the National Academy of Sciences, researchers at Harvard University in

31.
A) NO CHANGE
B) increased
C) increasing
D) had increased

32.
A) NO CHANGE
B) carbon, dioxide, methane
C) carbon dioxide, yet methane
D) carbon dioxide, methane

33.
A) NO CHANGE
B) sources
C) events
D) winners

34. Based on the graph provided in this selection, which of the following statements should be included at this point in the passage?

A) Although methane levels have balanced in the past, they continue to increase steadily.
B) Methane levels have continually decrease over the past 50 years.
C) Methane levels have reached a limit and cannot increase any further.
D) Although methane levels are interesting to research, they have no realistic meaning.

Cambridge, Massachusetts; Caltech in Pasadena, California; and NASA's Jet Propulsion Laboratory, also in Pasadena, suggest that methane emissions might not have increased dramatically in 2007 after all.

The researchers used long-term measurements of methane, [35] its isotopes and methyl chloroform (1,1,1,-trichloroethane, a chemical compound that serves as a proxy for estimating how long methane remains in the atmosphere) from numerous global ground stations. From [36] this data, the scientists were able to determine sources of methane and how quickly it is destroyed in Earth's atmosphere. They found that the most likely explanation for the recent increase has less to do with methane emissions than previously thought and more to do with changes in the availability of the hydroxyl radical (OH), which breaks down methane in the atmosphere. As such, the amount of hydroxyl in the atmosphere has an impact on global methane concentrations. If global levels of hydroxyl decrease, global methane concentrations will [37] increase — even if methane emissions remain constant.

"Think of the atmosphere like a kitchen sink with the faucet running," said co-corresponding author Christian Frankenberg, an associate professor of environmental science and engineering at Caltech and a JPL research scientist. "When the water level inside the sink rises, that can mean that you've

35.
A) NO CHANGE
B) its isotopes, but
C) its isotopes: and
D) its isotopes, and

36.
A) NO CHANGE
B) it is data
C) these data
D) have had data

37.
A) NO CHANGE
B) increase, even
C) increase. Even
D) increase/even

opened up the faucet more. Or it can mean that the drain is blocking up. You have to look at both."

In this analogy, the hydroxyl radical represents the draining mechanism in the sink. It is highly [38] remnant and acts like a detergent in the atmosphere, triggering a series of chemical reactions that culminate in the formation of carbon dioxide and water vapor.

In tracking the observed changes in methane and the inferred changes in hydroxyl, Frankenberg and [39] them noted that fluctuations in hydroxyl concentrations can explain some of the recent methane trends. However, the authors cannot explain the causes for the global changes in hydroxyl concentrations seen in the past decade. They say future independent studies are needed to quantify year-to-year variations in the hydroxyl radical and their potential drivers. They would also like to see the trends they detected verified with more detailed studies of the sources and the destruction mechanisms of methane, particularly in the tropics.

"The tropics are the tricky part," Frankenberg said. "They're very complex in terms of methane emissions and destruction." Methane has the shortest lifetime in the tropics due to the large amounts of water vapor and radiation there. But because tropical areas are often remote and cloud-covered (thwarting satellite observation), they remain understudied, he said.

38. Which of the following choices can replace the underlined word in order to further explain the properties of the hydroxyl radical?

A) NO CHANGE
B) reactive
C) resting
D) recuperating

39. To make this sentence less ambiguous, the author should replace the underlined word with which of the following?

A) NO CHANGE
B) them all
C) all of them
D) his colleagues

The study is titled "Ambiguity in the causes for decadal trends in atmospheric methane and hydroxyl." Frankenberg's collaborators on the paper are lead author and Harvard graduate student Alexander Turner, Daniel Jacob of Harvard, and Paul Wennberg of Caltech. 40 A NASA Carbon

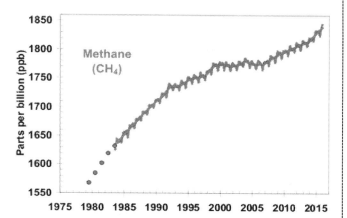

40. At this point the writer is considering adding the following statement:

Frankenburg and his collaborators really enjoyed studying trends in methane.

Should the writer make this addition here?

A) Yes, since it provides crucial information in support of the main idea of the passage
B) Yes, since it is a very interesting point made by the author
C) No, since it is an opinion that does not match the tone of the rest of the article
D) No, since the statement is not true

DIRECTIONS

For questions 1-10, solve each problem and choose the best answer from the choices provided. Fill in the corresponding circle on your answer sheet. For questions 11-13, solve the problem and bubble in your answer on the grid provided.

NOTES
- Calculator **is NOT allowed** in this section
- All variables and expressions represent real numbers unless otherwise indicated
- All figures are drawn to scale unless otherwise stated
- All figures lie in the same plane unless otherwise stated
- The domain of a given function is the set of all real numbers, unless otherwise stated

REFERENCE

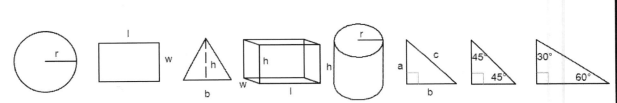

$A = \pi r^2$

$C = 2\pi r$

$A = l \cdot w$

$A = \dfrac{bh}{2}$

$V = lwh$

$V = \pi r^2 h$

$a^2 + b^2 = c^2$

Special Right Triangles

1. If $\frac{p}{2} = \frac{2p+2}{5}$, then $p =$

A) 2
B) 4
C) 5
D) 10

2. Solve for $x : \frac{(x \cdot 6 \div 3 + 2)}{3} = \frac{1}{3}$

A) $x = -\frac{1}{2}$

B) $x = \frac{1}{2}$

C) $x = \frac{1}{3}$

D) $x = -\frac{1}{3}$

3. Which of the following ordered pairs is a solution for the system shown below?

$$y = 2x + 3$$

$$y = 3x + 2$$

A) $(1,5)$
B) $(5,1)$
C) $(2,3)$
D) $(3,2)$

4. Which of the following is the solution to the inequality $-3x < -2x + 2$?

A) $x < -2$
B) $x < 2$
C) $x > 2$
D) $x > -2$

5. The cost of an adult ticket for a new amusement park is a dollars, and the cost of a children's ticket into a new amusement park is c dollars. Seniors can get into the park for free. Which of the following expresses the ticket cost for a family of 2 adults, 3 children, and 2 seniors?

A) $2c + 3a$
B) $2a + 3c$
C) $2a + 3a + 2s$
D) $2a + 3$

6. Five times the number of bears in a zoo is more than 4 times their number in the zoo plus 20. Which of the following could possibly be the number of bears in the zoo?

A) 18
B) 19
C) 20
D) 21

7.

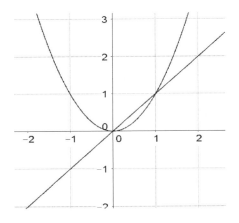

The graph above models the system:

$$y = x^2$$
$$y = x$$

Based on this information, how many solutions does the system have?

A) 0
B) 1
C) 2
D) None

8. If $y > 3$ and $x \leq -2$, which of the following is a possible solution for the system of inequalities?

A) $(-1, 4)$
B) $(4, -2)$
C) $(-2, 4)$
D) $(3, -2)$

The number of bacteria in an agar plate is shown in the table below:

Hour (h)	1	2	3	4
Bacteria count(b)	0	200	400	600

Questions 9 and 10 refer to the table shown above.

9. Which of the following is the appropriate linear model for the situation shown above?

A) $b = 200h - 200$
B) $b = 200h$
C) $b = 200h + 200$
D) $b = 2^h$

10. Using the table above, what is the best estimate for the number of bacteria in the plate during the tenth hour?

A) 1200
B) 1400
C) 1600
D) 1800

11. The amount of rainfall on Monday in New York is 2.25 inches, and the amount of rainfall in Los Angeles is 3.375 inches. Which of the following is the absolute difference between the amounts of rainfall in the two cities? Round your answer to the nearest hundredths place.

GRID IN

12. What is the smallest integer x for which the following inequality $125 - 5x < -10$ holds true?

GRID IN

13. What value of x satisfies both of the equations below?

$$|3x - 2| = 3$$
$$|6x - 10| = 0$$

Express your answer as a fraction reduced to the lowest terms.

GRID IN

Directions:

For questions 1-21, solve each problem and choose the best answer from the choices provided. Fill in the corresponding circle on your answer sheet. For questions 22-25, solve the problem and bubble in your answer on the grid provided.

Notes:

- Calculator **is allowed** in this section
- All variables and expressions represent real numbers unless otherwise indicated
- All figures are drawn to scale unless otherwise stated
- All figures lie in the same plane unless otherwise stated
- The domain of a given function is the set of all real numbers, unless otherwise stated

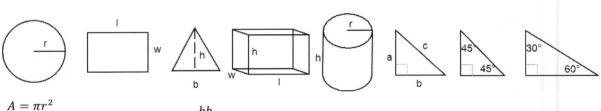

$A = \pi r^2$

$C = 2\pi r$

$A = l \cdot w$

$A = \dfrac{bh}{2}$

$V = lwh$

$V = \pi r^2 h$

$a^2 + b^2 = c^2$

Special Right Triangles

1. How many positive integers satisfy the inequality $\sqrt{x} < 4$?

A) 2
B) 4
C) 15
D) 16

2. The linear equation $4x + 2y = 16$ can be rewritten as:

A) $y = -2x + 8$
B) $y = 2x + 8$
C) $y = 4x + 16$
D) $y = -2x + 16$

3. When Amanda finished reading one-fifth of her new book, she had 480 pages remaining. How many pages are there in the entire book?

A) 180
B) 360
C) 600
D) 720

4. If the positive integer n is odd, then all of the following are even EXCEPT

A) $2n$
B) $2n + 1$
C) $2n + 2$
D) $2n + 6$

5. If 25 times a number equals the number plus 240, what is the value of 55% of the number?

A) 4
B) 4.5
C) 5
D) 5.5

6. Boyle's law states that pressure and volume are inversely proportional. A closed container with a volume of 5 liters has a pressure of 2 atm. What is the pressure of the container if the volume is doubled?

A) 1 atm
B) 2 atm
C) 5 atm
D) 10 atm

7. When a standard coin is flipped 3 times, what is the probability that it will land on heads at least twice?

A) $\frac{1}{8}$

B) $\frac{1}{4}$

C) $\frac{1}{2}$

D) $\frac{3}{4}$

8. Which of the following expresses the transformation when the function
$$y = (x + 3)^2 + 5$$
is shifted 3 units to the left and 3 units up?

A) $y = (x + 3)^2 + 2$
B) $y = (x)^2 + 8$
C) $y = (x)^2 + 2$
D) $y = (x + 6)^2 + 8$

9. The data shown in the scatterplot can best be described as having a

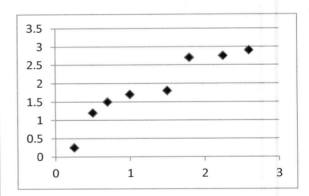

A) strong negative linear relationship
B) strong positive linear relationship
C) weak positive linear relationship
D) weak negative linear relationship

10. At a restaurant, there is a 10% chance that a waiter will receive a tip of 30 dollars. There is a 50% chance the waiter will receive a tip of 15 dollars, and there is a 40% chance that the waiter will receive a tip of 5 dollars. What is the expected value of tip money that a waiter will receive per night?

A) $10.00
B) $12.50
C) $15.00
D) $27.50

11. Joules Law states that in an electric circuit, $P = I^2 R$, where P is power, I is current, and R is the resistance. Which of the following represents the correct rearrangement of this equation when solving for the current?

A) $I = \frac{R}{p}$

B) $I = \frac{P}{R}$

C) $I = \frac{\sqrt{P}}{R}$

D) $I = \sqrt{\left(\frac{P}{R}\right)}$

12. Which of the following scenarios can best be described using a linear model?

A) The velocity of an accelerating car
B) The growth of cellular organisms
C) The amount of water that comes out of a hose pipe
D) The increase in human population

13. The graph of $f(x) = \frac{1}{\sqrt{x+3}}$ is undefined at which of the following values of x?

A) -3
B) -2
C) -1
D) 0

14. If $|x - 4| < 5$, which of the following could be the value of x?

A) -1
B) 3
C) 9
D) 11

Use the table below to answer questions 15-17.

Political Party Affiliation Survey Results from Orange County

Age	Pro-Republican	Pro-Democrat	None	Total
18-25	25	75	100	200
26-45	30	60	25	
46-65	48	57	96	201
Total	103	192	221	516

15. Based on the table above, which of the following is the number of people aged 26-45 who were surveyed in Orange County?

A) 103
B) 115
C) 200
D) 516

16. Given that a voter is aged 46-65, what is the probability that they are pro-republican? Round to the nearest hundredths place.

A) 0.09
B) 0.21
C) 0.24
D) 0.48

17. What is the probability that a randomly selected person from the survey above is Pro-Democrat and aged 18-25? Round to the nearest hundredths place.

A) 0.14
B) 0.15
C) 0.39
D) 0.61

18. The centripetal force of an object can be calculated using the formula $F = \frac{mv^2}{r}$, where F is the force in Newtons (N), m is the mass in kilograms (kg), v is the velocity in meters per second (ms^{-1}), and r is the distance from the center in meters (m). What is the centripetal force of an object with a mass of 5 kg moving at a speed of 10 meters per second, and a radius of 25 meters?

A) $10N$
B) $20N$
C) $30N$
D) $40N$

Math Test Scores

19. The scores obtained by students in a math test are shown in the scatterplot above. What is the average score for the test?

A) 72.5
B) 75.6
C) 76.3
D) 79.5

20. If $f(x) = x^2 + \frac{1}{x^2}$, then which of the following is equivalent to $f(2x)$?

A) $2x^2 + 2x + 2$

B) $2x^2 + \frac{1}{2x^2}$

C) $\frac{4x^2 + 2x^2}{x^2}$

D) $\frac{16x^4 + 1}{4x^2}$

21. When $5x^2 + 6x + 2$ is divided by $5x + 1$, the remainder is:

A) 1
B) $5x + 1$
C) $10x + 2$
D) $5x^2 + 2$

22. What value of c makes the quadratic function $f(x) = x^2 + 3x + c$ have exactly one solution?

GRID IN

24. One standard dice numbered 1-6 is rolled, and a coin is flipped at the same time. What is the probability that the number on the dice is prime AND the coin lands on heads? Express your answer as a decimal to the nearest hundredths place.

GRID IN

23. One scoop of vanilla ice cream and 3 scoops of chocolate ice cream cost $3.50, while 3 scoops of vanilla ice cream and 1 scoop of chocolate ice cream costs $4.50. What is the cost of 1 scoop of vanilla ice cream?

GRID IN

25. Let $g(x) = 5x^2 + 3x + 5$, and let $h(x) = 3x + 5$. What is the value of $g(h(2)) - g(3)$?

GRID IN

PRACTICE TEST 2 - ANSWERS- READING TEST

#	Explanations
1 B	The author repeatedly uses the phrase "when his ___." The repeated usage of a clause structure is also known as parallel structure, answer choice B.
2 A	Make sure to use context clues and synonyms while answering word choice questions. In the passage, the author states that Govinda had been partaking in discussions with wise men, meaning that he was involved in the discussions. This means that Govinda was participating in the discussions, answer choice A.
3 C	The passage states that the boy was "surrounded by the glow of the clear-thinking spirit" and that "He already knew to feel Atman..." These phrases indicate that Siddhartha is a religiously oriented child and has some special abilities, answer choice C.
4 B	Lines 18-24 provide evidence for the fact that Siddhartha was a child with a deep connection to his religions. These lines state that "he already knew how to speak the Om..." and that he was "surrounded by the glow of the clear-thinking spirit..." These phrases provide sufficient evidence to support the idea the Siddhartha was a pious and religious child.
5 B	Lines 27-35 state that Siddhartha would "become a great wise man and priest..." and that he was "strong and handsome." This supports the idea that Siddhartha is an ideal son and is fit to be king in the future, answer choice B.
6 A	The word luminous is used in line 39 to describe Siddhartha's forehead. This is a reference to the description of Siddhartha's forehead in lines 23-24, where it is described as "the forehead surrounded by the glow of the clear-thinking spirit." This indicates that his forehead was glowing, answer choice A.
7 C	From lines 1-70, the author praises Siddhartha and describes his achievements and amazing personality. Then in line 71, we can see that the author begins to describe the problems in Siddhartha's life in a conflicting manner, answer choice C.
8 A	The main idea of the passage is that Siddhartha was a perfect candidate to become the next king, but became restless at the thought of continuing his life. The main idea can be found by reading the beginning, middle, and end of this passage, which describe Siddhartha's shift from being crown prince to becoming restless, answer choice A.
9 D	In lines 4-9, the author states that "the enormous losses on all sides of the conflict resulted in part from...the failure of military leaders..." This provides evidence for the fact that the author places blame on the war's military leaders, answer choice D.
10 C	The information in lines 22-36 show that Wilson created the 14 Points Proposal to "bring about a just and lasting peace." This means that Wilson was willing to compromise with foreign countries to bring about peace in the world, answer choice C.

11 B	The word stringent is used in a way that shows Germany receiving a large punishment for being the chief instigator, or starter, of the large conflict. This means that the punishment was very strict and harsh, answer choice B.
12 B	The graphic shows that Germany and Russia had the highest amount of fatalities during the war. This information is supported by lines 46-47, where the author states that Germany was viewed as "the chief instigator of the conflict." The fact that Germany began the war helps explain why the number of German casualties was so high, answer choice B.
13 A	The passage states that Germany lost land gained from the Franco-Prussian war as well as many other areas of land gained in the past. These lands included large German populations and occupation, resulting in a very large loss for the Germans, answer choice A.
14 D	The creation of the War Guilt Clause allowed for the Allied powers to make sure that Germany's economy could not recover easily, thereby preventing another global scale conflict, answer choice D.
15 C	The reason for the creation of the War Guilt clause is that the French "greatly feared rapid German recovery and the initiation of a new war against France." The fact that Germany had to pay a huge amount of money avoided another conflict by limiting its ability to progress, answer choice C.
16 C	Line 87 states "the treaty restricted the Navy to vessels under 10,000 tons," meaning that the Navy cannot have more than 10,000 tons of vessels. This means that 10,000 tons is the limit created by the treaty, answer choice C.
17 B	Lines 1-4 state that the virus "probably" arrived in the Western Hemisphere from the Pacific, implying that the origin of the virus is not certain. The passage also states that more information was discovered about the origin of the virus after "a new genetic analysis of the epidemic," answer choice B.
18 D	In line 14, the word culprit is used to describe how the Zika virus led to the unexplained fever and skin rashes. This means that the Zika virus was confirmed as the cause, or perpetrator, for these symptoms, answer choice D.
19 D	The passage states the "World Health Organization did not declare the epidemic a public health emergency until February 2016, after babies of Zika-infected mothers began to be born with severe neurological problems." This means that the virus was only declared an emergency after many children were born with severe brain damage, answer choice D.
20 A	The evidence for the fact that Zika was declared as a public health emergency due to children being born with severe brain damage is found in lines 15-19, which describe the direct reason that the World Health Organization declared Zika as an emergency, answer choice A.
21 A	The passage states that study group 1 took a road trip across Brazil to "produce a complete catalog of the virus's genes," whereas study group 2 "estimated rate at which genetic changes appear, the scientists re-created Zika's evolutionary timeline." This means that the best answer choice is A.

22 B	The definition for the word undetected is "unable to be seen." In reference to the passage, the Zika virus passed around many countries without being detected, or secretly, answer choice B.
23 D	Pybus states "It's not immediately clear whether Zika stopped," implying that he is not certain about the path of the Zika virus. This phrase makes it evident that he is speaking with uncertainty, answer choice D.
24 C	The diagram clearly shows an increase in the number of children born with microcephaly after 2014. This can be correlated to the rise in mosquito populations as stated in Lines 75-77 in the passage, answer choice C.
25 C	In the final sentence, the passage states "Focusing on getting rid of mosquitoes is an effective way of preventing human cases," meaning that destroying mosquito populations is the most effective form of Zika prevention, answer choice C.
26 B	Randolph Bourne addresses intellectuals, colleagues, and the American public in general through his speech. Bourne tries to convey his point to society as a whole, labelling him as a social critic, answer choice B.
27 A	Bourne states "But the intellectual progress has been so gradual..." describing his lack of faith in the intellect of the American people. Additionally he states that " They would have thought anyone mad who talked of shipping American men by the hundreds of thousands..." highlighting the idea that he did not support the army sending troops overseas, answer choice A.
28 A	As used in line 40, the word sentiment is used to describe the war. This means that a sentiment is a type of feeling, or an attitude towards the war, answer choice A.
29 C	In the beginning of Wilson's speech, he states that "it was neither right nor constitutionally permissible that I should assume the responsibility of making," meaning that he believed that he was not powerful enough to declare war by himself, answer choice C.
30 B	In the final sentence of this excerpt, Wilson states that civilian boats "have been sunk with the same reckless lack of compassion or of principle." This implies that Wilson believes these attacks to be reckless and brash, answer choice B.
31 C	The first paragraph and last paragraph of this excerpt provide reasons for which Wilson thinks that Congress should push for war against the Germans. Some reasons include the Germans sinking ships containing civilians and the allies of the United States, answer choice C.
32 A	The arguments of the two passages are opposing each other, as Excerpt 1 is anti-war and Excerpt 2 is in support of the war, answer choice A.
33 A	Excerpt 1 is a social commentary provided to describe the author's argument against going to the war, whereas Excerpt 2 is a direct plea to the American Congress to join the war effort against Germany, answer choice A.

34 D	The statement that Burke makes comments on the unnecessary need to send American men overseas. The main argument of Wilson's speech is to send troops to defeat the Germans. Since these ideas are conflicting, Wilson would most likely argue against that fact that sending troops overseas is unnecessary, answer choice D.
35 D	The first line compares the monkey's brain building a human face to the structure of Mr. Potato Head. Since this is a comparison using "like" or "as," this sentence is using a simile, answer choice D.
36 A	The passage states that the monkey uses "about 200 cells that code for different sets of facial characteristics." This most directly relates to answer choice A.
37 B	The word "leading," as it is used in this sentence, describes the main scientific process by which primates recognize faces. This most directly relates to the word "primary," as this explanation is the primary reason for this scientific phenomenon, answer choice B.
38 D	The hyphen used in line 35 is followed by the words "for instance." This indicates that the information after the hyphen includes a specific example of a variable used in the statistical analyses, answer choice D.
39 B	Tsao states that the study "Was a total surprise." This means that the results of Tsao and Chang's experiment produced results that were not anticipated at the beginning, answer choice B.
40 D	The passage mainly employs the usage of these celebrities to show that the brain encodes differently for each of them. The passage states "You can build a specific lookup table that codes these into specific identities — like Barack Obama..." to show that there is a specific directory in the brain for this recognizable face, answer choice D.
41 A	The word concept, as it is used in the passage, is used as an antonym to the word "details". This means that a concept doesn't include the small details of a thought, but the big picture or the main idea, answer choice A.
42 B	The primary purpose of the passage is seen in lines 1-3 as well as in the last paragraph of the article. The article uses facts to inform the audience about a new way that brains recognize facial features, answer choice B.

PRACTICE TEST 2 – ANSWERS – WRITING AND LANGUAGE TEST

#	Explanation
1 B	A comma needs to be placed in between the two words in order to avoid a run on sentence. The comma helps separate the independent clauses of this sentence, answer choice B.
2 A	The additional sentence adds more details to the passage to highlight how exactly Gandhi has remained the same since 1920. This means that answer A is the correct choice.
3 D	The words saying, reciting, and speaking all mean the same thing. This means the author should only include one of these words to improve sentence flow. This reflects answer choice D.
4 D	The proper grammatical format when speaking is to always include the other object/person first. This means that Ahimsa should be before "I." Therefore the correct revision is "My Ahimsa and I," answer choice D.
5 D	Removing the underlined phrase makes the sentence less redundant, as Gandhi already used the phrase "nonviolent fight" in the same sentence, answer choice D.
6 D	The most effective way to combine these two sentences is to use a comma before the word "but," answer choice D.
7 D	The phrase "when it comes," is an interjection, and thus must be offset from the sentence using two commas, answer choice D.
8 A	The word "it's" is the same as "it is," which should not be used in this case. To indicate possession, the word "its" is correct, answer choice A.
9 C	Remember to always use a hyphen between the tens and ones place in a number. This means that a hyphen should be included in "twenty-two," answer choice C.
10 C	Sentence 5 discusses the "equal freedom for all." This means that it would make sense for the phrase "Everybody will be his own master" to come after the statements in sentence 5, answer choice C.
11 D	The best replacement for the underlined word is "you are." This will make the sentence read "When you sit down for breakfast, you are probably not thinking. The corresponding contraction for "you are" is "you're," answer choice D.
12 B	The graph shows that the current food supply of the Earth is growing at a faster rate than the population. This is partly because of the NASA satellites that provide observations of the food production, answer choice B.
13 D	The words "thrive," "grow," and "live" all have the same definition. This means that the best way to condense this sentence is to keep only one of these words in the sentence, answer choice D.

14 C	To improve the flow of the sentence, all of the items should be placed in one list. Additionally, there needs to be another comma before the word "and," answer choice C.
15 A	The additional statement allows for the audience to understand the meaning of the acronym SMAP. This means that the statement is a necessary addition that clarifies the meaning of this acronym, answer choice A.
16 C	The end of paragraph 7 introduces the observations made of soil moisture. Paragraph 6 provides more details on the soil moisture data. This means that paragraph 7 should be placed before paragraph 6 to provide continuity in the passage, answer choice C.
17 D	The subject of this sentence is the farmers, and the sentence deals with farmers deciding to change their practices in the future. This means that the word "their" should be changed to a tense that reflects the future. The best choice is to use "they will," or "they'll," answer choice D.
18 D	The sentence previously stated "could one day…" This implies that the simulations are for agricultural practices in the future. Therefore the phrase "in the future" doesn't have to be included again in the same sentence, answer choice D.
19 C	The only transition word given that indicates a contrast is "however." This transition word provides a contrast between the idea that the oceans have a lot of food and the idea that climate change is damaging the ecosystem, answer choice C.
20 D	The subject of this clause is the word "regions." Since this word is plural, to have proper subject verb agreement the verb must also be plural, meaning that the best choice is "are," answer choice D.
21 A	The two clauses of the sentence are best separated using a comma. This means that the sentence does not need revision, answer choice A.
22 B	The two sentences are contrasting. This means that the best way to combine them is to use the transition word "but," answer choice B.
23 B	The speaker is using a present tense to describe the affairs at home. This means that the best form of the word to use here would be "applies," answer choice B.
24 C	The author uses the word "search" in the same sentence as well as in the next sentence. This means that the author wishes for the audience to search their consciences, just like how he searches through his own, answer choice C.
25 A	To imply possession, the word "its" must be used. This means that the sentence does not require any further revision, answer choice A.
26 B	The sentence indicates that the men must respect their chiefs and obey them. This indicates that the men should be faithful to their superiors, answer choice B.
27 D	The best way to separate the two clauses of this statement is to use a comma, answer choice D.

28 C	The additional statement is a personal statement that does not have anything to do with military events. Due to this reason, it should not be included in the passage, answer choice C.
29 B	The phrase "that is to say, about 350,000 out of 400,000 men" is an interjection, or a piece of information set off from the rest of the passage. This means that it should be included within two hyphens before and after the information, answer choice B.
30 D	The main idea of the passage deals with military encounters. Additionally, the word "fiting" is misspelled in the passage. Therefore, the word should be replaced with "fighting" in order to make sense in the passage, answer choice D.
31 A	This sentence is written in the present tense and discusses the "recent" methane levels. This means that the verb "increases" should be in the present tense, which it already is. Therefore no further revision is needed, answer choice A.
32 D	The phrase "The second most important human-produced greenhouse gas after carbon dioxide" is used to describe methane. This means that it is a dependent clause that needs to be separated from the rest of the sentence using a comma, answer choice D.
33 B	This sentence describes the places that natural gas comes from. This is synonymous to the word "sources," answer choice B.
34 A	The graph shows that the methane levels have continually increased since 1975. The information in the passage also states that the methane emissions leveled off at some point in time. Combining these two pieces of information leads to the idea that although methane levels have leveled off in the past, they continue to increase steadily, answer choice A.
35 D	This sentence involves a list of items. This means that there should be a comma before the word "and" to adhere to proper grammatical rules, answer choice D.
36 C	Remember that the word "data" is plural. This means that the word that precedes it in this case should also be plural. The best fit in this sentence is "these data," answer choice C.
37 B	The best way to include the phrase "even if methane emissions remain constant" as an extra piece of information at the end of the sentence is to use a comma. This effectively sets off the phrase, answer choice B.
38 B	The second half of the sentence describes the hydroxyl radical as "triggering a series of chemical reactions..." This means that the chemical is very reactive, and a better replacement for the word "remnant" is "reactive," answer choice B.
39 D	The study mentioned in the passage is being done at Caltech, meaning that Dr. Frankenburg is working on this project with other fellow scientists. This means that the passage is most likely referring to his colleagues, answer choice D.
40 C	The statement is an opinion and is written in a more casual tone in comparison to the rest of the passage. For these reasons, it should not be included in the passage, answer choice C.

PRACTICE TEST 2 – ANSWERS – MATH TEST-No Calculator

#	Explanation
1 B	Cross multiplying gives: $$5p = 4p + 4$$ $$p = 4$$
2 A	$$\frac{(x \cdot 6 \div 3 + 2)}{3} = \frac{1}{3}$$ Since both of the denominators are 3, we can multiply the entire equation by 3 and simplify to eliminate the denominators. $$(x \cdot 2 + 2) = 1$$ $$2x + 2 = 1$$ $$2x = -1$$ $$x = -\frac{1}{2}$$
3 A	Since both of the equations are in terms of y, they can be set equal to each other: $$2x + 3 = 3x + 2$$ $$x = 1$$ Plugging back into one of the original equations to solve for y gives: $$y = 2(1) + 3 = 5$$ This means the ordered pair that satisfies the system is $(1,5)$.
4 C	$$-3x < -2x + 2$$ $$-3x + 2x < 2$$ $$-x < 2$$ Remember to reverse the sign in an inequality when multiplying or dividing by a negative number: $$x > 2$$

5 B	Since there are 2 adults, the cost of their tickets is $2a$. Since there are 3 children, the cost of their tickets is $3c$. The cost for seniors is zero. The total cost can be expressed as: $$2a + 3c$$
6 D	This scenario can be modeled by the inequality: $$5b > 4b + 20$$ Where b is the number of bears in the zoo. This inequality can be further simplified: $$b > 20$$ Since b must be greater than 20, the only possible answer choice that is greater than 20 is answer choice D.
7 C	The graph provided shows that there are two intersections between the line and the parabola. Alternatively, the system can be solved manually: $$x^2 = x$$ $$x^2 - x = 0$$ $$x(x - 1) = 0$$ $$x = 0, x = 1$$
8 C	We are looking for an ordered pair which has an x coordinate less than or equal to -2, and a y coordinate greater than 3. The only possible choice is the ordered pair $(-2,4)$, since the x value equals -2 and the y coordinate is greater than 3.
9 A	Using the table, we can derive the equation of a line using two of the data points: $(1,0)$ and $(2,200)$ $$\frac{200 - 0}{2 - 1} = 200$$ The slope of the line is 200, therefore $$b = 200h + y\ intercept$$ To solve for the y intercept, one of the original points can be plugged into the equation above: $$0 = 200(1) + y\ intercept$$ $$y\ intercept = -200$$ Therefore the entire linear equation is:

		$b = 200h - 200$
10 D		Plugging in $h = 10$ into the linear model from the previous question gives: $$b = 200(10) - 200$$ $$b = 2000 - 200$$ $$b = 1800$$
11 1.13		The absolute difference can be found using: $$|3.375 - 2.25| = 1.125 \ inches$$ Rounding this answer to the nearest hundredths place gives 1.13 $inches$
12 28		The inequality can be rewritten as: $$125 + 10 < 5x$$ $$135 < 5x$$ $$27 < x$$ This means that the smallest integer that is greater than 27 is 28.
13 5/3		Begin by solving the first equation: $$3x - 2 = 3$$ $$3x - 2 = -3$$ $$3x = 5$$ $$3x = -1$$ $$x = \frac{5}{3}, -\frac{1}{3}$$ We can plug in both of these values to test if they satisfy the second equation: $$\left|\frac{6 \cdot 5}{3} - 10\right| = 0$$ $$\frac{30}{3} - 10 = 0$$ $$10 - 10 = 0$$ This means that the value $x = \frac{5}{3}$ satisfies both equations.

PRACTICE TEST 2 – ANSWERS – MATH TEST-Calculator

#	Explanation
1 C	Squaring both sides gives: $$x < 16$$ This means that the numbers 1-15 satisfy the inequality, for a total of 15 positive integers
2 A	Since all of the answer choices are in the form $y =$, the equation needs to be rearranged in terms of y: $$2y = -4x + 16$$ $$y = -2x + 8$$
3 C	If $\frac{1}{5}$ of the book is read, then $\frac{4}{5}$ of the book is unread and consists of 480 pages: $$\frac{4}{5}x = 480$$ $$480 \cdot \frac{5}{4} = 600$$
4 B	Multiplying any integer by 2 will make it even. This means that adding an odd number to $2n$ will make it odd. The only answer choice where an odd number is being added to $2n$ is answer choice B.
5 D	This word problem can be rewritten as: $$25x = x + 240$$ $$24x = 240$$ $$x = 10$$ 55% of 10 is equal to $10 \cdot 0.55 = 5.5$
6 A	Since pressure and volume are inversely proportional, the product $pressure \cdot volume$ will always be equal to a constant value. Using the data provided in the question, the product of the pressure and volume is always $5 \cdot 2 = 10$. This means that if the pressure of the container is doubled to 10 liters, $10 \cdot pressure = 10$, and $pressure = 1\ atm$.
7 C	The cases that we are looking for out of three flips are: $$HHT, HTH, THH, HHH$$ The probability of getting exactly HHT is $\frac{1}{2} \cdot \frac{1}{2} \cdot \frac{1}{2} = \frac{1}{8}$ The probability of getting exactly HTH is $\frac{1}{2} \cdot \frac{1}{2} \cdot \frac{1}{2} = \frac{1}{8}$ The probability of getting exactly THH is $\frac{1}{2} \cdot \frac{1}{2} \cdot \frac{1}{2} = \frac{1}{8}$

	The probability of getting exactly HHH is $\frac{1}{2} \cdot \frac{1}{2} \cdot \frac{1}{2} = \frac{1}{8}$ The sum of these four probabilities is $\frac{1}{8} + \frac{1}{8} + \frac{1}{8} + \frac{1}{8} = \frac{4}{8} = \frac{1}{2}$
8 D	When the function is shifted 3 units to the left, the number 3 must be added to the inner expression. When the function is shifted up 3 units, the number 3 must be added to the constant value outside the parentheses: $$y = (x + 6)^2 + 8$$
9 B	The line of best fit for the data is shown below: Since the data points are very close to the line of best fit, there is a strong linear relationship. Additionally the slope of the line of best fit is positive, meaning that there is a strong positive linear relationship.
10 B	Expected value relates to a weighted average. The calculation of the weighted average is: $$\frac{\big((10 \cdot 30) + (50 \cdot 15) + (40 \cdot 5)\big)}{100} = \$12.50 \; per \; night$$
11 D	In this formula, we are trying to isolate and solve for I: $$\frac{P}{R} = I^2$$ $$I = \sqrt{\left(\frac{P}{R}\right)}$$
12 C	Answer choice A is non-linear since the velocity of the car does not increase at a constant rate as the acceleration increases. Answer choice B is non-linear as cellular organisms grow at an exponential rate. Answer choice D is also non-linear for the reason that humans do not populate at a linear rate. Answer choice C is a linear situation, as the water from the hose pipe is constant and will fill up a container at a linear rate.

13 A	When $x = -3$, the denominator of the fraction becomes 0. This makes the overall fraction equal to $\frac{1}{0}$, making the function undefined. Additionally the graph of the function shows that there is no value at $x = -3$: 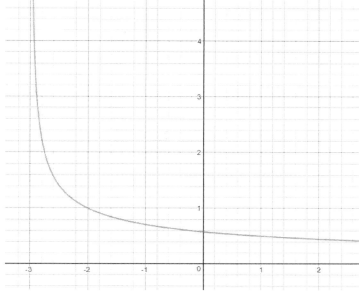
14 B	The absolute inequality can be rewritten as: $$-5 < x - 4 < 5$$ $$-1 < x < 9$$ The only answer choice between -1 and 9 is answer choice B.
15 B	The number of people aged 25-46 who were surveyed is equal to the sum of the numbers in the row labeled 25-46. This is equal to $30 + 60 + 25 = 115$
16 C	The total number of people who are aged 46-65 is 201. Out of these 201, 48 are Pro-republican. This means that the probability is: $$\frac{48}{201} = 0.24$$

17 B	To find the AND probability, look for the overlapping region:

<table>
<tr><th>Age</th><th>Pro-Republican</th><th>Pro-Democrat</th><th>None</th><th>Total</th></tr>
<tr><td>18-25</td><td>25</td><td>75</td><td>100</td><td>200</td></tr>
<tr><td>26-45</td><td>30</td><td>60</td><td>25</td><td></td></tr>
<tr><td>46-65</td><td>48</td><td>57</td><td>96</td><td>201</td></tr>
<tr><td>Total</td><td>103</td><td>192</td><td>221</td><td>516</td></tr>
</table>

This means that out of the 516 people who were surveyed, 75 of them are Pro-Democrat AND aged 18-25. This gives a probability of:

$$\frac{75}{516} = 0.15$$

18 B	The information given in the problem is:

$$m = 5, v = 10, and\ r = 25$$

Plugging into the equation provided gives:

$$F = \frac{(5)(10^2)}{25} = \frac{500}{25} = 20N$$

19 C	Since the plot shows frequency on the y-axis, we read the information as "5 people got a 55 on the test." Therefore the total sum of all the scores is:

$$(55 \cdot 5) + (65 \cdot 3) + (70 \cdot 5) + (80 \cdot 7) + (95 \cdot 4) + (100 \cdot 3) = 2060$$

There are a total of $5 + 3 + 5 + 7 + 4 + 3 = 27$ students. The average score is $\frac{2060}{27} = 76.3$

20 D	Plugging in $2x$ into the equation gives:

$$(2x)^2 + \frac{1}{(2x)^2}$$

$$4x^2 + \frac{1}{4x^2}$$

$$\frac{16x^4}{4x^2} + \frac{1}{4x^2}$$

	$$\frac{16x^4 + 1}{4x^2}$$
21 A	Long division of the polynomials gives: $$\begin{array}{r} x \\ 5x+1\overline{)5x^2 + 6x + 2} \\ -(5x^2 + x) \\ \hline 0 + 5x + 2 \\ -(5x + 1) \\ \hline \boxed{1} \end{array}$$
22 9/4 or 2.25	For a quadratic equation to have exactly one solution, the value $b^2 - 4ac$ must equal zero. In this case, $a = 1, b = 3,$ and c is unknown. Therefore: $$9 - 4c = 0$$ $$9 = 4c$$ $$c = \frac{9}{4} = 2.25$$
23 5/4 or 1.25	Let vanilla = x, and chocolate =y: $$x + 3y = 3.50$$ $$3x + y = 4.50$$ Solving the equations simultaneously gives: $$-3x - 9y = -10.50$$ $$3x + y = 4.50$$ $$-8y = -6.00$$ $$y = 0.75$$ Plugging back into the original equation to solve for x: $$x + 3(0.75) = 3.50$$ $$x + 2.25 = 3.50$$ $$x = 1.25$$

24 ¼ or 0.25	For the dice to be prime, it must land on a 2, 3, or 5. This means that there is a $\frac{1}{2}$ chance that the dice is prime. There is a $\frac{1}{2}$ probability that the coin lands on heads. Since this is an AND probability scenario, we can multiply the two independent probabilities. $\frac{1}{2} \cdot \frac{1}{2} = \frac{1}{4}$
25 584	$$h(2) = 3(2) + 5 = 11$$ $$g(11) = 5(11)^2 + 3(11) + 5 = 5 \cdot 121 + 33 + 5 = 605 + 33 + 5 = 643$$ $$g(3) = 5(3)^2 + 3(3) + 5$$ $$= 5 \cdot 9 + 9 + 5 = 45 + 14 = 59$$ $$643 - 59 = 584$$

Questions 1-8 are based on the passage below.

Passage 1

Read the following excerpt from Things Fall Apart by Chinua Achebe and answer the questions that follow.

(1)   Okonkwo was well known throughout the nine villages and even beyond. His fame rested on solid personal achievements. As a young man of eighteen he had brought honor

(5) to his village by throwing Amalinze the Cat. Amalinze was the great wrestler who for seven years was unbeaten, from Umuofia to Mbaino. He was called the Cat because his back would never touch the earth. It was this man that

(10) Okonkwo threw in a fight which the old men agreed was one of the fiercest since the founder of their town engaged a spirit of the wild for seven days and seven nights. The drums beat and the flutes sang and the spectators held

(15) their breath. Amalinze was a wily craftsman, but Okonkwo was as slippery as a fish in water. Every nerve and every muscle stood out on their arms, on their backs and their thighs, and one almost heard them stretching to breaking

(20) point. In the end Okonkwo threw the Cat. That was many years ago, twenty years or more, and during this time Okonkwo's fame had grown like a bush-fire in the Harmattan.

    He was tall and huge, and his bushy

(25) eyebrows and wide nose gave him a very severe look. He breathed heavily, and it was said that, when he slept, his wives and children in their houses could hear him breathe. When he walked, his heels hardly touched the ground

(30) and he seemed to walk on springs, as if he was going to pounce on somebody. And he did pounce on people quite often. He had a slight stammer and whenever he was angry and could not get his words out quickly enough, he would

(35) use his fists. He had no patience with unsuccessful men. He had had no patience with his father.

    Unoka, for that was his father's name, had died ten years ago. In his day he was lazy

(40) and improvident and was quite incapable of thinking about tomorrow. If any money came his way, and it seldom did, he immediately bought gourds of palm-wine, called round his neighbors and made merry. He always said that

(45) whenever he saw a dead man's mouth he saw the folly of not eating what one had in one's lifetime. Unoka was, of course, a debtor, and he owed every neighbor some money, from a few cowries to quite substantial amounts.

(50)   He was tall but very thin and had a slight stoop. He wore a haggard and mournful look except when he was drinking or playing on his flute. He was very good on his flute, and his happiest moments were the two or three

(55) moons after the harvest when the village musicians brought down their instruments, hung above the fireplace. Unoka would play with them, his face beaming with blessedness and peace. Sometimes another village would

(60) ask Unoka's band and their dancing Egwugwu to come and stay with them and teach them their tunes. They would go to such hosts for as long as three or four markets, making music and feasting. Unoka loved the good hire and the

(65) good fellowship, and he loved this season of the year, when the rains had stopped and the sun rose every morning with dazzling beauty. And it was not too hot either, because the cold and dry Harmattan wind was blowing down from

(70) the north.

    Some years the Harmattan was very severe and a dense haze hung on the atmosphere. Old men and children would then sit round log fires, warming their bodies. Unoka

(75) loved it all, and he loved the first kites that returned with the dry season, and the children who sang songs of welcome to them. He would

remember his own childhood, how he had often wandered around looking for a kite sailing
(80) leisurely against the blue sky. As soon as he found one he would sing with his whole being, welcoming it back from its long, long journey, and asking it if it had brought home any lengths of cloth.

1. Which of the following best describes the reason for Okonkwo's widespread fame?
A) His ability to tame a cat
B) His fierceness as a warrior and fighter
C) His cold-blooded attitude towards other humans
D) His ability to harvest the greatest amount of crops in the summer

2. The simile used in lines 15-16 ("but...water") help convey the message that

A) The Cat was able to capture Okonkwo as easily as a fish out of water
B) Okonkwo used the power of the fish that he consumed to defeat the Cat
C) Okonkwo was able to dodge attacks while fighting, similar to the way a fish is slippery in water
D) The slippery adaptations of a fish allowed Okonkwo to defeat his opponent

3. The word "hardly" in line 29 most nearly means:

A) Significantly
B) Barely
C) Unwillingly
D) Constantly

4. Lines 35-37 ("He...father") uses parallel structure to imply that:

A) Okonkwo's father was an unsuccessful man
B) Okonkwo supported his father's life decisions
C) Okonkwo only tolerated his father because they lived in the same village
D) Okonkwo did not have a father and wished that he had one

5. Okonkwo's father, Unoka, can best be described as
A) Judgmental
B) Cautious
C) Greedy
D) Thoughtless

6. A physical difference between Okonkwo and his father is that

A) Okonkwo was short, whereas his father was tall
B) Okonkwo was well built, whereas his father was very frail
C) Okonkwo wore glasses, whereas his father wore contact lenses
D) Okonkwo saved his money, whereas his father spent it all

7. Which choice most effectively supports the answer to the previous question?

A) Lines 24-26 ("He...look) and Lines 50-51 "(He...stoop")
B) Lines 31-32 ("And...often") and Lines 53-55 ("He...harvest")
C) Lines 36-37 "(He...father") and Lines 57-59 ("Unoka...peace)
D) Lines 41-43 ("If...wine") and Lines 62-64 ("They...feasting")

8. The main idea of this passage is that

A) Okonkwo tried his best to follow in his father's footsteps, but failed in the process
B) Okonkwo looked up to his father, Unoka, as he became the greatest warrior in the village
C) Okonkwo and his father, Unoka, led contrasting lives with different purposes and goals
D) Okonkwo was a rebellious child who did not listen to his father, Unoka

Questions 9-17 are based on the passage below.

Passage 2

Read the following 1974 speech titled "What Educated Women Can Do" by Indira Gandhi and answer the questions that follow.

(1)   An ancient Sanskrit saying says, woman is the home and the home is the basis of society. It is as we build our homes that we can build our country. If the home is inadequate -
(5) either inadequate in material goods and necessities or inadequate in the sort of friendly, loving atmosphere that every child needs to grow and develop - then that country cannot have harmony and no country which does not
(10) have harmony can grow in any direction at all.
        That is why women's education is almost more important than the education of boys and men. We -- and by "we" I do not mean only we in India but the entire world -- have
(15) neglected women education. It is fairly recent. Of course, not to you but when I was a child, the story of early days of women's education in England, for instance, was very current. Everybody remembered what had happened in
(20) the early days.
        I remember what used to happen here. I still remember the days when living in old Delhi even as a small child of seven or eight. I had to go out in a doli* if I left the house. We
(25) just did not walk. Girls did not walk in the streets. First, you had your sari with which you covered your head, then you had another shawl, or something with which you covered your hand and all the body, then you had a
(30) white shawl, with which everything was covered again although your face was open fortunately. Then you were in the doli, which again was covered by another cloth. And this was in a family or community which did not
(35) observe segregation by gender of any kind at all. In fact, all our social functions always were mixed functions but this was the atmosphere of the city and of the country.

Now, we have got education and there (40) is a debate all over the country whether this education is adequate to the needs of society or the needs of our young people. I am one of those who always believe that education needs a thorough overhauling. But at the same time, I (45) think that everything in our education is not bad, that even the present education has produced very fine men and women, specially scientists and experts in different fields, who are in great demand all over the world and even (50) in the most affluent countries. Many of our young people leave us and go abroad because they get higher salaries; they get better conditions of work.

But it is not all a one-sided business (55) because there are many who are persuaded and cajoled to go even when they are reluctant. We know of first class students, especially in medicine or nuclear energy for instance, they are approached long before they have (60) graduated and offered all kinds of incentives to go out. Now, that shows that people do consider that they have a standard of knowledge and capability which will be useful anywhere in the world.

Primary School Attendance Rate in India, 2005

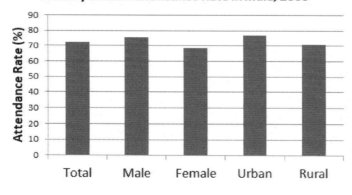

(65)   So, that is why I say that there is something worthwhile. It also shows that our own ancient philosophy has taught us that nothing in life is entirely bad or entirely good. Everything is somewhat of a mixture and it (70) depends on us and our capability how we can extract the good, how we can make use of what is around us. There are people, who through

observation, can learn from anything that is around them. There are others, who can be (75) surrounded by the most fascinating people, the most wonderful books, and other things, and who yet remain quite closed in and they are unable to take anything from this wealth around them.

*Doli: A small enclosed carriage

9. Which of the following is the argument of the author, as expressed in paragraph 1?

A) Ancient Sanskrit phrases are more important than the current state of women in India
B) Since women are the basis of society, they need to be more active in the government
C) Women are required to remain at home and take care of children
D) Women require sufficient resources in order to allow the country to progress as a whole

10. The author introduces which of the following in paragraph 3?

A) Simile
B) Anecdote
C) Metaphor
D Personification

11. The speaker repeatedly uses the word "covered" in paragraph 3 in order to:
A) Explain the reason for her upbringing in severe poverty as a child
B) Persuade the audience to cover themselves before walking outside
C) Introduce an appeal to humor that would make her speech more interesting
D) Convey the message that girls in India did not have complete freedom in the past

12. The transition between paragraphs 3 and 4 (Lines 38 and 39) can best be described as:

A) Happy to Sad
B) Depressed to Enlightened
C) Past to Present
D) Present to Future

13. The word "affluent" in line 50 most nearly means:

A) Wealthy
B) Interesting
C) Fluent
D) Poor

14. Based on the information in the passage, a valid inference is that

A) Indira Gandhi does not believe that women will be able to be educated in the future
B) Indira Gandhi believes that ancient philosophies have valid meaning in the present day
C) Indira Gandhi believes that Indian education should receive more funding
D) Indira Gandhi does not believe that Indian infrastructure is sufficient to educate the masses

15. Which choice most effectively supports the answer to the previous question?

A) Lines 61-64 ("Now...world")
B) Lines 65-66 ("So...worthwhile")
C) Lines 66-68 ("It...good")
D) Lines 69-72 ("Everything...us")

16. The graphic included in the passage supports which of the following statements?

A) The total number of female Indian students is much greater than the number of male Indian students.
B) Females in India are no longer allowed to receive an education.
C) A majority of female children in India are able to receive a proper education.
D) Due to increased funding, more females are able to study than males.

17. The word "fascinating" in line 75 most nearly means:

A) Interesting
B) Depressing
C) Repressed
D) Enrolling

Questions 18-25 are based on the passage below.

Passage 3

Read the following article detailing a new improvement in medicinal technology and answer the questions that follow.

(1)   Keeping a cool attitude helps when handling an accident victim who has lost a large amount of blood. But keeping patients cool might also help, a new study finds. It might save
(5)   their lives.

Here's why: Losing a lot of blood can lead to a dangerous loss of blood pressure. That can limit how much blood, and therefore oxygen, reaches the brain and other vital
(10)organs. If deprived of enough oxygen, those tissues — and the patient — could die.

The body doesn't have to spill most of its blood for this to happen. Losing about 2 liters (a half gallon) out of the 5 liters (1.3
(15)gallons) or so in the body could be fatal. In fact, most deaths among army troops are due to excess blood loss — even if the inflicted wounds do not directly affect a vital organ, says Victor Convertino. A physiologist, he studies body
(20)functions at a research institute of the U.S. Army in Houston, Texas. He was not involved in this study.

Convertino thinks medics and others can save some lives if they can maintain
(25)adequate blood pressure — and thereby blood flow — to vital tissues until the victim reaches the hospital. (Vital tissues include the heart and brain.) Once there, blood transfusions can take over.

(30)   Blair Johnson may have found a way to achieve this. He is a physiologist at the University of Buffalo in New York. There, he focuses on developing effective ways to maintain blood pressure in the body after
(35)potentially catastrophic blood loss. He described a potential new first-aid approach to cope with such situations, April 26, at the Experimental Biology meeting in Chicago, Ill. His idea is simple: Just cool the victim's face.

(40)   Johnson drew inspiration from the body's natural response to a drop in the supply of oxygen to its tissues. Consider when you dive into a swimming pool. The body abides by a simple rule: When in crisis, save the vital
(45)organs. So, while underwater, the body turns on a so-called "diving reflex." It directs to the brain and heart what limited oxygen is available. "Your blood pressure goes up, and your heart rate falls down, especially if the water is cold,"
(50)Johnson explains.

Think of blood vessels as a system of fluid-filled tubes. When the body is exposed to cold water, these tubes narrow. If the fluid volume stays the same, the overall pressure in
(55)the system increases.

Cooling the entire body of an accident victim is impractical. But cooling just the face should be possible, says Convertino — even when dealing with injuries on the battlefield.

(60)   To test the idea, Johnson's group recruited 10 people to take part in an experiment. None had to actually lose blood. Instead, the scientists tricked their bodies into believing that they had. To do this, they sealed
(65)each person's body from the waist down in a chamber. Then a vacuum sucked air out of the chamber. This dropped the pressure inside. Blood rushed to the lower body of the volunteers because of the pressure difference
(70)between the chamber and rest of the room. This mimics how the body reacts to losing about 1 liter (0.3 gallon) of blood.

While the machine simulated blood loss, the researchers treated the recruits' faces.
(75)They placed a bag containing a mix of either ice and water or just water onto the forehead and over the eyes. Placing the cold ice-water bag on the face of volunteers for 15 minutes increased blood pressure, the scientists found. In fact, it
(80)pushed blood pressure close to normal. This treatment also decreased the volunteers' heart rate. Placing a bag of only water on the face of volunteers, though, did not affect their blood pressure and heart rate.

(85)   This face-cooling treatment is not a long-term fix, Convertino cautions. It is likely to help most when a hospital can be reached

within 15 minutes. "If it gets past 30 to 60 minutes, it may not be so practical," he says. (90) After that time, the tissues may begin experiencing too much oxygen loss and die.

18. According to the information in the passage, which of the following is needed by the human body to function?

A) A cold temperature
B) A cool attitude
C) Oxygen
D) A dangerous loss of blood

19. Which of the following is a job description of a physiologist?

A) One who helps people heal through treatment
B) One who studies how the body works
C) One who discovers cures for diseases
D) One who immediately responds to calls of distress

20. The word "transfusions" in line 28 most nearly means:

A) Transfers
B) Positions
C) Transformations
D) Mechanisms

21. It can most reasonably inferred from the information in lines 30-39 ("Blair...face") that:

A) Johnson will never be able to prove that his idea works
B) Johnson is not fit to be a physiologist or a doctor
C) Johnson's idea has not been fully developed yet
D) Johnson was not the first person to develop this new idea

22. Which of the following does NOT occur when the human body is submerged underwater?

A) Blood Pressure increases
B) Heart rate falls down
C) The oxygen flow in the body completely stops
D) The body turns on the "diving reflex"

23. The study outlined in lines 60-84 is included in the passage to:

A) Persuade the audience that face cooling is the best way to save a bleeding victim
B) Entertain the audience with a new study performed on humans
C) Prove that Johnson is always correct in his scientific methods of thinking
D) Prove that face-cooling is an effective method of decreasing heart rate during blood loss

24. The passage implies that Johnson's new method of face-cooling:

A) Is a long-term solution for fixing blood loss and heart attacks
B) Is best used while the victim is being transported to the hospital
C) Is the best way to cure cancerous tissues that increase blood loss
D) Helps prevent cardiac arrest in patients

25. Which choice most effectively supports the answer to the previous question?

A) Lines 73-74 ("While...faces")
B) Lines 80-82 ("This...rate")
C) Lines 85-86 ("This...cautions")
D) Lines 86-88 ("It...minutes")

Questions 26-33 are based on the passage below.

Passage 4
Read the following speech by Patrick Henry from March 1775 and answer the questions that follow.

(1)   No man thinks more highly than I do of the patriotism, as well as abilities, of the very worthy gentlemen who have just addressed the House. But different men often see the same

(5) subject in different lights; and, therefore, I hope it will not be thought disrespectful to those gentlemen if, entertaining as I do opinions of a character very opposite to theirs, I shall speak forth my sentiments freely and without reserve.

(10)   This is no time for ceremony. The question before the House is one of awful moment to this country. For my own part, I consider it as nothing less than a question of freedom or slavery; and in proportion to the

(15) magnitude of the subject ought to be the freedom of the debate. It is only in this way that we can hope to arrive at truth, and fulfill the great responsibility which we hold to God and our country. Should I keep back my opinions at

(20) such a time, through fear of giving offense, I should consider myself as guilty of treason towards my country, and of an act of disloyalty toward the Majesty of Heaven, which I revere above all earthly kings.

(25)   Mr. President, it is natural to man to indulge in the illusions of hope. We are apt to shut our eyes against a painful truth, and listen to the song of that siren till she transforms us into beasts. Is this the part of wise men,

(30) engaged in a great and arduous struggle for liberty? Are we disposed to be of the number of those who, having eyes, see not, and, having ears, hear not, the things which so nearly concern their temporal salvation? For my part,

(35) whatever anguish of spirit it may cost, I am willing to know the whole truth, to know the worst, and to provide for it.

   I have but one lamp by which my feet are guided, and that is the lamp of experience. I

(40) know of no way of judging of the future but by

the past. And judging by the past, I wish to know what there has been in the conduct of the British ministry for the last ten years to justify those hopes with which gentlemen have been
(45) pleased to solace themselves and the House. Is it that insidious smile with which our petition has been lately received?

Trust it not, sir, it will prove a snare to your feet. Suffer not yourselves to be betrayed
(50) with a kiss. Ask yourselves how this gracious reception of our petition comports with those warlike preparations which cover our waters and darken our land. Are fleets and armies necessary to a work of love and reconciliation?
(55) Have we shown ourselves so unwilling to be reconciled that force must be called in to win back our love?

Let us not deceive ourselves, sir. These are the implements of war and subjugation, the
(60) last arguments to which kings resort. I ask gentlemen, sir, what means this martial array, if its purpose be not to force us to submission? Can gentlemen assign any other possible motive for it? Has Great Britain any enemy, in this
(65) quarter of the world, to call for all this accumulation of navies and armies? No, sir, she has none. They are meant for us, they can be meant for no other. They are sent over to bind and rivet upon us those chains which the British
(70) ministry has been so long forging. And what have we to oppose to them? Shall we try argument? Sir, we have been trying that for the last ten years.

26. Patrick Henry uses the first paragraph of the passage to tell his audience that:

A) He wishes to begin the war against the British for American freedom
B) He is a very intelligent man and therefore the audience should believe his statements
C) Although he is a patriotic man, the remainder of his speech may be offensive to the audience
D) He is willing to fight for the American people until they achieve a victory

27. The passage implies that

A) Henry is a Loyalist who supports the British taxation in the United States
B) Henry believes that the British are treating the Americans like slaves
C) Henry is a patriotic man, but prefers to keep the country in isolation
D) Henry would be a great future president of the United States

28. Which choice most effectively supports the answer to the previous question?

A) Line 10 ("This...ceremony")
B) Lines 10-12 ("The...country")
C) Lines 12-14 ("For...slavery")
D) Lines 16-19 ("It...country")

29. The word "illusions" in line 26 most nearly means:

A) Fantasies
B) Realities
C) Corrections
D) Events

30. Henry uses which of the following techniques in lines 38-39?

A) Idiom
B) Allusion
C) Personification
D) Persuasion

31. Henry uses a series of rhetorical questions in paragraph 5 in order to

A) Provide a set of questions that he will answer later in the speech
B) Ask the audience a series of questions to test their knowledge
C) Propose a series of questions that make the audience question their existence
D) Make the audience question the reasons for the recent British involvement in America

32. According to Henry, the new British fleets and armies present in American territory can be considered as

A) a boost for the American economy
B) a form of slavery
C) an act of war
D) a usage of spies in the war

33. The primary purpose of this passage is to

A) prove that the Americans can negotiate with the British
B) argue for the war against the British
C) evaluate the pros and cons of a war with the British
D) explain the results of the American Revolution

Questions 34-42 are based on the excerpts below.

Passage 5

Excerpt 1

Read the following excerpt highlighting the positives of stem cell research.

(1)   The people who favor embryonic stem cell research are mostly scientists, and they have many arguments. The first of these arguments is called utilitarianism, which is
(5) about how the benefits of stem cell research outweigh the ethical problem of destroying embryonic life. An example of utilitarianism is that embryonic stem cells have the capacity to grow a lot in a lab and can differentiate into
(10) almost all types of bodily tissue. This makes embryonic stem cells a good source for cellular therapies to treat many diseases. Also the social, economic and personal costs of the diseases that embryonic stem cells can cure are
(15) far greater than the costs associated with the destruction of embryos.
        Another argument for research of stem cells retrieved from embryos is human potential and humanity, which is a similar argument to
(20) utilitarianism. The argument of humanity is about how embryos are not technically life when they are inside the womb, but instead are merely potential for life. Also, the argument says that a blastocyst, which changes into an
(25) embryo, is a group of human cells that have not differentiated into anything yet, making cells of the inner cell mass no more "human" than a skin cell. Another thing that the scientists who favor stem cell research say is that the ends
(30) (saving people who are already living) justify the means (killing things that are not alive yet).
        The final argument used by those who would like to advance the research of embryonic stem cells is superiority, that
(35) embryonic stem cells can be considered a lot better therapeutically than adult stem cells. Embryonic stem cells are easier to grow into

cultures; they divide quicker, and they are much more abundant than adult stem cells, not to
(40) mention that embryonic stem cells can treat a wider range of diseases than adult stem cells. There are just as many arguments against embryonic stem cells as there are for, but the biggest question is the grey area between
(45) where human life begins, whether it is in a fertilized egg, in the womb, or when the fetus can survive independently from the mother.

Excerpt 2

Read the following excerpt stating the negatives of stem cell research and answer the questions that follow.

There just as many people against stem cells research as there are for it. These people
(50) range from politicians, especially right wing politicians, to scientists, to religious people. One of these people's biggest arguments against stem cells is the value of life. This argument in the highly controversial stem cell
(55) debate is based on the belief that an embryo is actually human, and that it should be treated just like human life, and this happens as soon as an egg is fertilized.

Another argument is that there are better
(60) alternatives to embryonic stem cells. Embryonic stem cells should be abandoned in favor of alternatives like adult stem cells, and pro-life supporters say that the use of adult stem cells from sources such as umbilical cord blood has
(65) consistently produced more promising results than the use of embryonic stem cells. This argument directly contradicts the pro-embryonic stem cell argument about how embryonic stem cells are superior to adult stem
(70) cells. Adult stem cell research will prosper if it gets the money currently going to embryonic stem cells, the pro-life supporters point out.

The final argument for the people against embryonic stem cells research is the scientific
(75) flaws that could be involved with the use of embryonic stem cells in therapies. One concern with embryonic stem cell treatments is that sometimes stem cells from embryos can create

tumors. The bottom line of this argument is that
(80) stem cells may not be as good as some scientists say they are. The main issue of this raging debate is whether potential embryonic life should be treated the same way as you or me.

Politics in Stem Cell Research

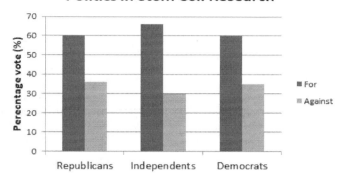

34. According to the first passage, stem cell research is important for scientists due to the fact that

A) Stem cells are able to differentiate into any type of bodily tissue
B) Stem cells originate from embryos
C) Stem cells are magical organisms that grow in the early stages of human development
D) Stem cell research is well funded, and scientists are required to spend the money given to them

35. Which of the following describes the role of a blastocyst?

A) A form of stem cell research done by specialized scientists
B) A lump of cells that transforms into the human embryo
C) A single skin cell on the embryo of a human
D) A potential for life in the womb

36. Which of the following is a reason that embryonic stem cells are more useful than adult stem cells?

A) Embryonic stem cells are less abundant than adult stem cells
B) Embryonic stem cells cannot divide quickly in comparison to adult stem cells
C) Embryonic stem cells are weaker than adult stem cells
D) Embryonic stem cells have the ability to treat more diseases than adult stem cells

37. The word "controversial" in line 54 most nearly means:

A) Interesting
B) Compromising
C) Arguable
D) Extraordinary

38. Which of the following is true about pro-life supporters according to Excerpt 2?

A) Pro-life supporters prefer that scientists research adult stem cells instead of embryonic stem cells
B) Pro-life supporters want scientists to receive more money to research embryonic stem cells
C) Pro-life supports do not like scientists researching new cures for diseases
D) Pro-life supporters wish to change the way adult stem cells are extracted

39. The audience of Excerpt 2 is most likely

A) Highly educated scientists
B) Government officials
C) The general public
D) The author's family

40. The diagram above shows that a majority of the members of the Republican Party will agree with the argument made in which excerpt?

A) Excerpt 1
B) Excerpt 2
C) Both Excerpts 1 and 2
D) Neither Excerpt 1 nor 2

41. Which choice best states the relationship between the two excerpts?

A) Excerpt 1 challenges the primary argument of Excerpt 2
B) Excerpt 1 is proven to be more accurate than Excerpt 2
C) Excerpt 1 supports the main argument of Excerpt 2
D) Excerpt 2 is an expansion of Excerpt 1

42. The debate between Excerpt 1 and Excerpt 2 can be best categorized as:

A) Logical
B) Ethical
C) Emotional
D) Promotional

Questions 1-10 are based on the following passage.

Men and Women:

What is patriotism? Is it love of [1] ones birthplace, the place of childhood's recollections and hopes, dreams and aspirations? Is it the place where, in childlike naiveté, we would watch the passing clouds, and wonder why we, too, could not float so swiftly? The place where we would [2] counted the milliard glittering stars, terror-stricken lest each one "an eye should be," piercing the very depths of our little souls? Is it the place where we would listen to the music of the birds and long to have wings to fly, even as they, to distant lands? Or is it the place where we would sit on Mother's knee, enraptured by tales of great deeds and [3] conquests. In short, is it love for the spot, every inch representing dear and precious recollections of a happy, joyous and playful childhood?

If that were patriotism, few American men of today would be called upon to be patriotic, since the place of play has been turned into factory, mill, and mine, while deepening sounds of machinery have replaced the [4] music, sounds, and tones of the birds. No longer can we hear the tales of great deeds, for the stories our mothers tell today are but those of sorrow, tears and grief.

1.
A) NO CHANGE
B) one is
C) ones's
D) one's

2.
A) NO CHANGE
B) counting
C) will count
D) count

3.
A) NO CHANGE
B) conquests?
C) conquests!
D) conquests"

4.
A) NO CHANGE
B) music, and sounds, tones
C) music and tones
D) music

What, then, is patriotism? "Patriotism, sir, is the last resort of scoundrels," said Dr. Samuel Johnson. Leo Tolstoy, the greatest anti-patriot of our [5] time, defines patriotism as the principle that will justify the training of wholesale murderers; a trade that requires better equipment in the exercise of man-killing than the making of such necessities as shoes, clothing, and houses; a trade that guarantees better returns and greater glory than that of the honest workingman.

Indeed, conceit, [6] arrogance and egotism are the essentials of patriotism. Let me illustrate. Patriotism assumes that our globe is divided into little spots, each one surrounded by an iron gate. Those who have had the fortune of being born on some particular spot consider themselves nobler, better, grander, more intelligent than those living beings inhabiting any other spot. It is, therefore, the duty of everyone living on that chosen spot to fight, kill and die in the attempt to impose his superiority upon all the others. [7]

The inhabitants of the other spots reason in like manner, of course, with the result that from early infancy the mind of the child is provided with blood-curdling stories about the Germans, the French, the Italians, Russians, etc. When the child has reached manhood he is thoroughly saturated with the belief that he is chosen by the Lord himself to defend his country against the attack or invasion of any foreigner. It is for that purpose that

5.
A) NO CHANGE
B) time:
C) time;
D) time.

6.
A) NO CHANGE
B) arrogance; and egotism
C) arrogance, and egotism
D) arrogance. And egotism

7. At this point the writer is considering adding the following statement:

> Most people are not patriotic to their country and should go to jail for this reason.

Should the writer make this addition here?

A) Yes, as it provides crucial information about the future of patriotism
B) Yes, as it provides an opinion that that supports the main idea
C) No, as it presents an opinion that does not relate to the main idea of the passage
D) No, as it introduces unnecessary humor to the passage

we are [8] bargaining for a greater army and navy, more battleships and ammunition.

[1] To make them more attractive and acceptable, hundreds and thousands of dollars are being spent for the display of toys. [2] That was the purpose of the American government in equipping a fleet and sending it along the Pacific coast, that every American citizen should be made to feel the pride and glory of the United States. [3] An army and navy represent the people's toys. [9]

The city of [10] san francisco spent one hundred thousand dollars for the entertainment of the fleet; Los Angeles, sixty thousand; Seattle and Tacoma, about one hundred thousand. Yes, two hundred and sixty thousand dollars were spent on fireworks, theater parties, and revelries, at a time when men, women, and children through the breadth and length of the country were starving in the streets; when thousands of unemployed were ready to sell their labor at any price.

8. The author wished to replace the underlined word with one that indicates a sense of urgency. Which of the following is the best replacement?

A) NO CHANGE
B) pressing
C) negotiating
D) walking

9. For the sake of cohesion, sentence 3 should be placed:

A) NO CHANGE
B) before sentence 1
C) after sentence 1
D) removed from the passage

10.
A) NO CHANGE
B) san, francisco
C) San Francisco
D) San: Francisco

Questions 11-20 are based on the following passage.

Start counting. In the time it takes you to reach 10, 25 acres of the [11] worlds rain forests will be destroyed. That's the size of 20 football fields, and that has scientists alarmed. What's all the fuss?

"The rain forest is home to millions of plants and animal species that are not found anywhere else in the world, from tiny creatures like beetles and spiders to elephants, tigers, and chimpanzees," says Diane Jukofsky of the Rainforest Alliance in [12] Moravia Costa Rica.

Although the world's rain forests cover just 7 percent of land on Earth, they're home to more than 50 percent of all known animal and plant species, says [13] Jukofsky? Most are located in Latin America, Africa, and Asia. Unlike regular forests, rain forests receive at least 100 inches of rain a year, which supply animals with an abundance of food and shelter.

[1] Rain forests also provide an ideal climate for vegetation to thrive. [2] Some trees reach 200 feet tall. [3] These towering giants form a canopy high above the ground. [4] Rain forests are fun places to explore for adults and children alike. [14]

11.
A) NO CHANGE
B) world's
C) worlds's
D) world is

12.
A) NO CHANGE
B) Moravia: Costa Rica
C) Moravia, Costa Rica
D) DELETE the underlined phrase

13.
A) NO CHANGE
B) Jukofsky!
C) Jukofsky:
D) Jukofsky.

14. For the sake of cohesion, which sentence in this paragraph should be removed?

A) NO CHANGE
B) Sentence 2
C) Sentence 3
D) Sentence 4

"Rain forests are ever green," says Jukofsky. "Things are always blooming and growing in the rain forest. You'll find these very [15] nice trees. It's kind of like walking through a cathedral. All above you is a beautiful mass of green."

Many of the medicines now used to treat illnesses and diseases come from plants that [16] growed in the rain forest. In fact, one in four prescriptions sold at pharmacies comes from flowering plants. Of those, one in three are rain-forest plants.

But today, the world's rain forests are in danger. More than half have been destroyed. As the destruction [17] continues, scientists fear the world's remaining 2.5 billion acres may soon disappear. The culprit? Humans.

Like animals, millions and millions of people around the world rely on the rain forest for food and shelter. In many cases, families clear or burn an area of the forest for farming. [18] They plant crops for a couple of seasons before moving on to a new spot in the forest. Entire forests have been cut down and converted into pastures for cattle ranching. Mineral-rich forests have also been demolished for mining.

15. The writer wishes to replace the underlined word with another that will help improve the flow of the paragraph. Which of the following is the best replacement?

A) NO CHANGE
B) tall
C) boring
D) sad

16.
A) NO CHANGE
B) growing
C) grow
D) grew

17.
A) NO CHANGE
B) continues- scientists
C) continues: scientists
D) continues scientists

18. At this point the writer is considering adding the following sentence based on the diagram shown below:

   A majority of the forest land in Central America is used for small farming.

Should the writer make this addition here?

A) Yes, because this sentence supports the idea that many families rely on the rain forest
B) Yes, because it is an interesting piece of information
C) No, because it does not support the main idea of the passage
D) No, because it is too persuasive to include in this passage

So what's being done to stop the world's shrinking forests from vanishing altogether? Conservation groups across the globe are lobbying to preserve the forests. In Brazil, the World Bank and the World Wildlife Fund International are working with government officials to put 10 percent of the Brazilian Amazon Forest under government [19] protection. And organizations like the Rainforest Alliance regularly inspect forests for damage.

Jukofsky says kids can pitch in, too, by buying products marked with rain forest-friendly labels.

"All of us can do something to save rain forests," she says. "Since so many products come from Latin America, Africa, and Asia—from furniture to bananas—we can make sure that what we buy [20] doesnt hurt the forests that grow on these continents."

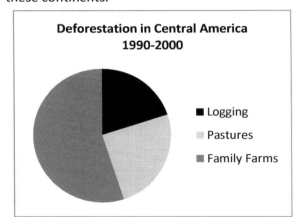

Deforestation in Central America 1990-2000

- Logging
- Pastures
- Family Farms

19.
A) NO CHANGE
B) protection and
C) protection, and
D) protection: and

20.
A) NO CHANGE
B) doesnit
C) does'nt
D) doesn't

Questions 21-30 are based on the following passage.

[1]

Friends and fellow citizens: I stand before you tonight under indictment for the alleged crime of having voted at the last presidential election, without having a lawful right to vote. It shall be my work this evening to prove to you that in thus voting, I not only committed no crime, but, instead, simply exercised my [21] citizens rights, guaranteed to me and all United States citizens by the National Constitution, beyond the power of any state to deny.

[2]

The preamble of the Federal Constitution says: We, the people of the United States, in order to form a more perfect union, establish justice, insure domestic tranquility, provide for the common defense, [22] promote the general welfare and secure the blessings of liberty to ourselves and our posterity, do ordain and establish this Constitution for the United States of America.

[3]

It was we, the people; not we, the white male citizens; nor yet we, the male citizens; but we, the whole people, who [23] thought the Union. And we formed it, not to give the blessings of liberty, but to secure them; not to the half of ourselves and the half of our posterity, but to the whole people - women as well as men. And it is a downright mockery to talk to women of their enjoyment of the blessings of liberty while they

21.
A) NO CHANGE
B) citizens's
C) citizen's
D) citizen

22.
A) NO CHANGE
B) promote the general welfare; and secure the blessings of liberty to ourselves
C) promote the general welfare, and secure the blessings of liberty to ourselves
D) promote the general welfare: and secure the blessings of liberty to ourselves

23.
A) NO CHANGE
B) created
C) destroyed
D) hoped

are denied the use of the only means of securing them provided by this democratic-republican government -- the ballot.

[4]

For any state to make gender a qualification that must ever result in the disfranchisement of one entire half of the people, is to pass a bill of attainder, or, an ex post facto law, and is therefore a [24] violation, offense, and misconduct of the supreme law of the land. [25]

[5]

The only question left to be settled now is: Are women [26] persons. And I hardly believe any of our opponents will have the hardihood to say they are not. Being persons, then, women are citizens; and no state has a right to make any law, or to enforce any old law, that shall abridge their privileges or immunities. Hence, every discrimination against women in the constitutions and laws of the several states is today null and void.

24.
A) NO CHANGE
B) violation and offense and misconduct
C) violation and offense
D) violation

25. At this point the writer is considering adding the following sentence:

> By it the blessings of liberty are forever withheld from women and their female posterity.

Should the writer make this addition here?

A) Yes, because it is a very persuasive statement
B) Yes, because it highlights the future consequences of making gender a qualification for voting
C) No, because most women already had the right to vote
D) No, because the author is not a female and is actually a male

26.
A) NO CHANGE
B) persons!
C) persons:
D) persons?

[6]

To them this government has no just powers derived from the consent of the governed. To them this government is not a democracy. It is not a republic. It is an odious aristocracy, the most hateful aristocracy ever established on the face of the globe; an oligarchy of 27 wealth, where the rich govern the poor. An oligarchy of learning, where the educated govern the ignorant, or even an oligarchy of race, where the Saxon rules the African, might be endured; but this 28 patriatchy, which makes father, brothers, husband, sons, the oligarchs over the mother and sisters, the wife and daughters, of every household - which ordains all men sovereigns, all women subjects, 29 carried dissension, discord, and rebellion into every home of the nation. Webster, Worcester, and Bouvier all define a citizen to be a person in the United States, entitled to vote and hold office. 30

27.
A) NO CHANGE
B) wealth
C) wealth; where
D) wealth: where

28.
A) NO CHANGE
B) partiartchy
C) patriartchy
D) patriarchy

29.
A) NO CHANGE
B) carry
C) carries
D) will carry

30. For the sake of cohesion, paragraph 5 should be placed:

A) NO CHANGE
B) before paragraph 1
C) after paragraph 2
D) after paragraph 6

Questions 31-40 are based on the following passage.

For the first time, researchers have successfully sequenced the DNA from Egyptian mummies. The findings reveal that these ancient people were more genetically similar to populations living in the eastern Mediterranean [31] — a region that today includes Syria, Lebanon, Israel, Jordan, and Iraq — than people living in modern-day Egypt.

"We were excited to have at hand the first genome-wide data of ancient Egyptian [32] mummies" said Stephan Schiffels, leader of the Population Genetics Group at the Max Planck Institute for the Science of Human History, in Jena, Germany.

Schiffels and a team of scientists from Poland, Germany, England, and Australia led by Johannes Krause, [33] a geneticist at the also Max Planck Institute for the Science of Human History, published their research in the May 30 issue of the journal Nature Communications.

Worldwide, the remains of thousands of mummies from ancient Egypt have been [34] excavated, but obtaining intact, undamaged DNA from the bodies has proved challenging.

31.
A) NO CHANGE
B) a region that today includes Syria, Lebanon, Israel, Jordan, and Iraq
C) :a region that today includes Syria, Lebanon, Israel, Jordan, and Iraq
D) ;a region that today includes Syria, Lebanon, Israel, Jordan, and Iraq;

32.
A) NO CHANGE
B) mummies;"
C) mummies:"
D) mummies,"

33.
A) NO CHANGE
B) a geneticist at also the Max Planck Institute
C) also a geneticist at the Max Planck Institute
D) a geneticist also at the Institute Max Planck

34. Which of the following is the best way to separate these two sentences?

A) NO CHANGE
B) excavated. And
C) excavated. However
D) excavated. Likewise

"Researchers were generally skeptical about DNA preservation in Egyptian mummies, due to the hot climate, the high humidity levels in [35] tombs and some of the chemicals used during mummification, which are all factors that make it hard for DNA to survive for such a long time," Schiffels told Live Science.

Other research teams made at least two previous attempts to sequence DNA from mummies, but those efforts were met with [36] some skepticism. The first undertaking occurred in 1985 and was later shown to be flawed, because the samples had become contaminated with modern DNA. The second analysis, published in 2010, focused on King [37] Tutankhamun's family, but it could not satisfy the critics either. Both studies [38] use a technique called polymerase chain reaction (PCR), which can hone in on specific fragments of genetic information but can't distinguish ancient DNA from modern DNA, nor differentiate human DNA from other types that may be present.

In this latest study, Krause and his colleagues used a newer technique called next-generation sequencing, which can extract human DNA from other types and can tell whether a genetic fragment is very old or suspiciously new (an indication that it might be modern).

35.
A) NO CHANGE
B) tombs-and
C) tombs but
D) tombs, and

36. The author wishes to replace the underlined word with one that describes the large amount of skepticism surrounding the research. Which of the following is the best replacement?

A) NO CHANGE
B) intense
C) sarcastic
D) interrupting

37.
A) NO CHANGE
B) Tutankhamuns
C) Tutankhamuns'
D) Tutankhamun;s

38.
A) NO CHANGE
B) used
C) using
D) will use

The scientists focused their efforts on the heads of 151 mummified individuals who lived in the settlement of Abusir el-Meleq, south of Cairo, and were buried between 1380 B.C. and A.D. 425.

[39] There, they irradiated the surfaces of bone and soft tissue for 60 minutes using ultraviolet radiation, which destroyed any modern DNA. The scientists then removed samples from inside soft tissue, skull bones and the tooth pulp.

Following these and numerous other rigorous steps, the researchers found that the soft tissues had no viable DNA. However, the bone and tooth samples for 90 individuals contained ample amounts of DNA from mitochondria, the organelles inside a cell that convert oxygen and nutrients into energy. Mitochondrial DNA is passed down from mother to child and so contains genetic information from only the mother's side of the family. [40]

39. At this point the writer is considering adding the following sentence:

> To reduce the risk of contamination, the researchers extracted the DNA inside a laboratory clean room.

Should the writer make this addition here?

A) Yes, as it is introduces information found in the following sentence
B) Yes, as it provides crucial information about the composition of DNA found in the study
C) No, as it does not help support the argument of the passage
D) No, as it is too humorous and does not match the tone of the passage

40. Which of the following is the topic sentence of this paragraph?

A) Viable DNA can never be extracted from Egyptian mummies
B) Soft tissues are useless for scientific analysis
C) Bone and tooth samples from Egyptian mummies contain valuable genetic material
D) Only the mother's side of the family can pass down genetic material

DIRECTIONS

For questions 1-10, solve each problem and choose the best answer from the choices provided. Fill in the corresponding circle on your answer sheet. For questions 11-13, solve the problem and bubble in your answer on the grid provided.

NOTES

- Calculator **is NOT allowed** in this section
- All variables and expressions represent real numbers unless otherwise indicated
- All figures are drawn to scale unless otherwise stated
- All figures lie in the same plane unless otherwise stated
- The domain of a given function is the set of all real numbers, unless otherwise stated

REFERENCE

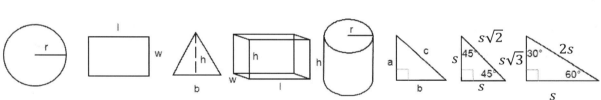

$A = \pi r^2$

$C = 2\pi r$

$A = l \cdot w$ $A = \dfrac{bh}{2}$ $V = lwh$ $V = \pi r^2 h$ $a^2 + b^2 = c^2$ Special Right Triangles

1. If $2x + 3 = 3x - 2$, what is the value of x?

A) 2
B) 3
C) 4
D) 5

2. Bob drove 6 hours at a speed of 60 miles per hour. If he still needed to drive 120 miles after this time, how far away was his destination?

A) 120
B) 240
C) 480
D) 720

3. The amount of money in a bank account increases by a compounded rate of 20 percent per year. If the account started with $100, how much money will it have after 2 years?

A) $120
B) $140
C) $144
D) $156

4. Which of the following is a solution to the following inequality?
$$3d + 2 < 6$$

A) $\frac{3}{4}$

B) $\frac{4}{3}$

C) $\frac{5}{3}$

D) 3

5. Car A travels at a rate of 50 miles per hour. Car B travels at a rate of 60 miles per hour. If Car A started off 300 miles in front of Car B, how many hours will it take for the cars to meet?
A) 10 hours
B) 20 hours
C) 30 hours
D) 40 hours

6. Which of the following linear equations models a situation where a person who weighs 120 pounds gains 7 pounds a year? Let y represent years and w represent weight.

A) $120 = 7y + w$
B) $w = 120 + 7y$
C) $y = 7w + 120$
D) $120y = 7w + y$

Questions 7-8 are based on the graph below.

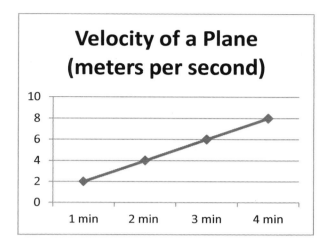

Velocity of a Plane (meters per second)

7. Which of the following is the numerical value of the slope of the graph above?
A) 1
B) 2
C) 3
D) 4

8. Which of the following is the numerical difference between the velocity of the plane at 4 minutes and the velocity of the plane at 3 minutes?

A) 1
B) 2
C) 4
D) 8

9. The amount of water in a reservoir increases at a rate of 1000 gallons every even numbered year and decreases at a rate of 500 gallons every odd numbered year. How much water did the reservoir gain from 2008-2016?
A) 1000
B) 2000
C) 3000
D) 5000

10. A commercial private jet flies 6 miles above the Earth's surface. A nuclear submarine travels 1 mile beneath the Earth's surface. What is the absolute difference between the two heights?

A) 5
B) 6
C) 7
D) 8

11. How many solutions does the following system have?

$$5x + 6y = 7$$
$$10x + 12y = 8$$

GRID IN

12. In their first season, a baseball team has won 3 games and lost 4 games. How many more games does the team need to win in a row to have a 5:2 win/loss ratio?

GRID IN

13. How many positive integer solutions exist for the inequality below?

$$5x + 3 < 2(x - 2) + 15$$

GRID IN

DIRECTIONS

For questions 1-21, solve each problem and choose the best answer from the choices provided. Fill in the corresponding circle on your answer sheet. For questions 22-25, solve the problem and bubble in your answer on the grid provided.

NOTES

Calculator **is allowed** in this section
- All variables and expressions represent real numbers unless otherwise indicated
- All figures are drawn to scale unless otherwise stated
- All figures lie in the same plane unless otherwise stated
- The domain of a given function is the set of all real numbers, unless otherwise stated

REFERENCE

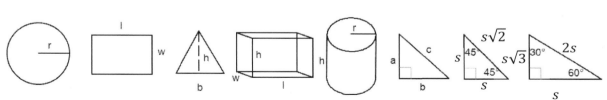

$$A = \pi r^2$$
$$C = 2\pi r$$
$$A = l \cdot w \qquad A = \frac{bh}{2} \qquad V = lwh \qquad V = \pi r^2 h \qquad a^2 + b^2 = c^2 \qquad \text{Special Right Triangles}$$

1. If $3^{-x} = 9$, then what is the value of x?

A) -3
B) -2
C) -1
D) 2

2. The expression $3(x + 2) = 3y$ can be simplified as:

A) $y = x + 2$
B) $y = 3x + 2$
C) $3y = x + 6$
D) $y = 3x + 5$

3. Emily donated 35% of her last month's paycheck to charity, which totaled 300 dollars. How much is Emily's monthly paycheck?

A) $105.00
B) $857.14
C) $1000.00
D) $1258.79

Use the graph provided to answer questions 4-5

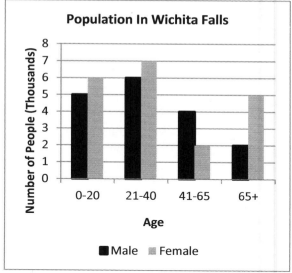

4. The double bar graph above shows the age distribution of people in Wichita Falls. In which of the following age group is the difference between the number of the male and females the greatest?

A) 0-20
B) 21-40
C) 41-65
D) 65+

5. How much greater is the population of the 21-40 year olds in comparison to the 0-20 year olds?

A) 0
B) 1,000
C) 2,000
D) 3,000

6. There are 3 roads from Tim's house to the city library. There are 5 roads from the library to Tim's school. How many total paths can Tim take from his house to school, if he has to go through the library?

A) 3
B) 5
C) 8
D) 15

7. Coulomb's law sates the force of attraction between two charges is represented by the equation:

$$F = k \cdot \frac{q_1 \cdot q_2}{r^2}$$

Which of the following represents this equation after the variable r is isolated?

A) $r = \sqrt{\left(\frac{k \cdot q_1 \cdot q_2}{F}\right)}$

B) $r = \frac{k \cdot q_1 \cdot q_2}{F}$

C) $r = \sqrt{\frac{q_1 \cdot q_2}{F}}$

D) $r = k \cdot q_1 \cdot q_2 \cdot F$

8.

x	2	4	6	8
$f(x)$	3	7	11	15

Based on the table above, which of the following is the value of $f(13)$?

A) 13
B) 17
C) 25
D) 26

9. John takes 4 hours to mow a lawn, whereas Jeffrey takes 7 hours to mow the same lawn. If they both work together on one lawn, how long will it take them to finish?

A) 3 *hours*

B) 11 *hours*

C) $\frac{28}{11}$ *hours*

D) $\frac{11}{28}$ *hours*

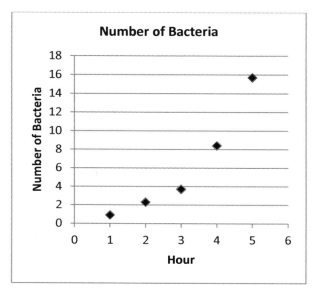

Number of Bacteria

10. The line of best fit for the data above can best be described as?

A) Linear
B) Exponential
C) Cubic
D) Horizontal

11. Which of the following functions best describes the relationship between the time (t) in hours and the number (n) of bacteria?

A) $n = 3t + 5$
B) $n = t^2$
C) $n = 2^t$
D) $n = 2t^2 + 2t + 1$

12. If $|3x - 5| < 23$, which of the following is a possible value of x?

A) 0
B) 10
C) 21
D) 28

13. The function $f(x) = (x - 2)^2 + 6$ is shifted 37 units down. What is the equation of the resulting function?

A) $f(x) = (x + 35)^2 + 6$
B) $f(x) = (x - 39)^2 + 6$
C) $f(x) = (x - 2)^2 + 31$
D) $f(x) = (x - 2)^2 - 31$

14. The sum of the number of cows and chickens on a farm is greater than 25, and the number of legs of the cows and chickens is less than 100. Which of the following could be the number of cows and chickens on the farm?

A) 30 cows, 10 chickens
B) 25 cows, 0 chickens
C) 20 cows, 5 chickens
D) 10 cows, 20 chickens

Use the table provided below to answer questions 15-17.

Survey of Favorite Sport in Fremont High School

	Soccer	Football	Total
Boys	10		
Girls		5	
Total		25	80

15. The table above shows partial information about the favorite sport for 80 students surveyed. How many girls were surveyed in total?

A) 10
B) 25
C) 35
D) 50

16. If a boy is chosen at random, what is the probability that football is his favorite sport?

A) $\frac{1}{3}$

B) $\frac{2}{3}$

C) $\frac{1}{4}$

D) $\frac{3}{4}$

17. Based on the table above, what is the ratio of girls who like soccer to boys who like football?

A) 1:2
B) 3:2
C) 4:6
D) 9:4

18. The equation to calculate the force F of an object in Newtons (N), is given by $F = m \cdot a$, where m is the mass of an object, and a is its acceleration. Additionally, the acceleration of the object can be calculated using the formula $a = \frac{v}{t}$, where v is the velocity of the object, and t is the time the object travels. Based on this information, what is the force of an object with a mass of 2kg traveling at a velocity of 5 meters per second for 10 seconds?

A) 0.5N
B) 1.0N
C) 1.5N
D) 2.0N

19. If $f(x) = 3x^2$, and $g(x) = 2x + 5$, which of the following expresses $f(g(x))$?

A) $3 \cdot (2x + 5)^2$
B) $6x^2 + 5$
C) $3x^2 + 2x + 5$
D) $x^2 + 5$

20.
$$y = x^4$$
$$y = 16$$

How many solutions does the above system have?

A) 0
B) 1
C) 2
D) 4

21. A regular dice numbered 1-6 is rolled 3 times in a row. What is the probability that the dice lands on the same number all three times?

A) $\frac{1}{216}$

B) $\frac{1}{36}$

C) $\frac{1}{6}$

D) $\frac{1}{2}$

22. A car travels for 3 hours at a speed of 80 miles per hour. Then the car does not move for 5 hours. Finally, the car travels for another 6 hours at a speed of 40 miles an hour. What is the car's average speed over the entire 14 hours? Express your answer to the nearest tenths place.
GRID-IN

23. How many positive integer solutions does the inequality $\frac{|2x+7|}{5} < 3$ have?
GRID-IN

24. If z is an integer such that $-17 \leq z \leq 3$, and k is an integer such that $-2 \leq k \leq 5$, what is the largest possible value of $z \cdot k$?
GRID-IN

25. If the equation $\sqrt{x+2} = 2x + 3$ is written in the form of $ax^2 + bx + c = 0$, what is the sum of $a + b + c$?
GRID-IN

PRACTICE TEST 3 - ANSWERS- READING TEST

#	Explanation
1 B	The evidence for this question can be found in lines 9-12, which state "It was this man that Okonkwo threw in a fight which the old men agreed was one of the fiercest since the founder of their town ..." This sentence shows that Okonkwo was able to defeat a skilled warrior, helping him achieve fame as a fighter in his village, answer choice B.
2 C	The passage uses the simile to show a comparison between Okonkwo and his ability to fight like a fish. This uses the idea that fish are very slippery and hard to catch to convey the message that Okonkwo was a skilled fighter, answer choice C.
3 B	Line 29 provides a description of the way that Okonkwo walks, and describes him as walking on springs. This means that his heels would not touch the ground very often, indicating that his heels barely touched the ground, answer choice B.
4 A	Lines 35-37 state "He had no patience with unsuccessful men. He had had no patience with his father." This implies that since Okonkwo does not have patience with unsuccessful men or his father, he considered his father an unsuccessful man, answer choice A.
5 D	Paragraph 3 describes Unoka as a man who was lazy and never saved his money like a wise man. This shows that Unoka was a very thoughtless father, answer choice D.
6 B	Line 24 states that Okonkwo was "tall and huge," and line 50 states that his father was "tall but very thin." This means that the physical difference between Okonkwo and his father is that Okonkwo was well built, whereas his father was very thin, answer choice B.
7 A	As stated in the answer to the previous question above, the physical difference between Okonkwo and Unoka is described in Line 24 and Line 50, showing that Okonkwo was well built whereas his father was very thin, answer choice A.
8 C	This passage highlights the differences between the lives of Okonkwo and his father. We can see an indication of this contrast in lines 35-37, where the author conveys the fact that Okonkwo did not look up to his father due to his foolishness, answer choice C.
9 D	The speaker states that women and children need to grow and develop in order for the country to "grow in any direction at all," answer choice D.
10 B	The speaker begins to use the 1st person beginning in paragraph 3 to describe an instance that she was oppressed as a child. This means that the speaker is using an anecdote, or a short story, to convey her message, answer choice B.
11 D	The author repeatedly uses the word "covered" in paragraph 3 to describe how she had to enclose herself in clothes before leaving her house. This shows that girls in India were not given freedom, and were required to follow strict guidelines, answer choice D.

12 C	In paragraph 3, the speaker presents an anecdote from her past as a child. In paragraph 4, the speaker presents her views on current education. Additionally the transition word "now" in line 39 indicates a shift from the past to the present, answer choice C.
13 A	Lines 44-53 describe how the Indian education system has produced scientists and experts who are in demand all across the world. This means that they are even in demand in countries that have more money than India, or wealthier countries, answer choice A.
14 B	The last paragraph of the speech states that "ancient philosophy has taught us that nothing in life is entirely bad or entirely good." The speaker's reference to this ancient philosophy implies that she believes that this idea has a valid meaning in the present day, answer choice B.
15 C	The best evidence for the inference that Gandhi believes in the meanings of ancient philosophies can be found in lines 66-68, which state "It also shows that our own ancient philosophy has taught us that nothing in life is entirely bad or entirely good," answer choice C.
16 C	The graph of primary school attendance rates in India shows that about 68% of Indian girls are able to receive some form of education. Since this is a majority of the female population in India, the correct answer is C.
17 A	The word fascinating is used in the passage to describe a group of people as very intelligent or interesting, answer choice A. This answer can also be derived from the fact that the sentence in lines 75-76 includes the word "wonderful," meaning that the descriptions in this sentence are positive.
18 C	In paragraph 1, the passage states that if the body is "deprived of enough oxygen, those tissues — and the patient — could die." This means that the body requires oxygen to survive, answer choice C.
19 B	The passage states that "...A physiologist, he studies body functions." This means that the best description of a physiologist is one who studies the mechanics of the body, answer choice B.
20 A	The word transfusion is used to describe the process that occurs to the blood once the victim reaches the hospital. This means the best synonym for a transfusion is a transfer, answer choice A.
21 C	Lines 30-39 use words like "may have" in line 30 and "potential new first-aid approach" in line 36 to show that Johnson's new idea is not completely proven to be successful, answer choice C.
22 C	From lines 40-50, the passage states that "So, while underwater, the body turns on a so-called "diving reflex." It directs to the brain and heart what limited oxygen is available. "Your blood pressure goes up, and your heart rate falls down, especially if the water is cold." This means that answer choice A, B, and D all occur when the body is under water.
23 D	The study outlined in the passage describes how patients reacted to a cool bag of water when their brains were tricked into believing that they had lost blood. This was primarily included to prove the point made by Johnson, that cooling the face of a bleeding victim would help

	maintain blood pressure and heart rate, answer choice D.
24 B	Lines 86-88 state, "It is likely to help most when a hospital can be reached within 15 minutes," meaning that the face cooling technique outlined by Johnson works best for a short term duration on the way to a hospital, answer choice B.
25 D	Lines 86-88 state "It is likely to help most when a hospital can be reached within 15 minutes," meaning that the new method of face-cooling works best while the victim is being transported to the hospital, answer choice D.
26 C	Henry uses the first passage as a warning to the listeners of his speech that "I hope it will not be thought disrespectful to those gentlemen..." Henry warns the audience that his ideas are different than that of the people, even though he is still a very patriotic man, answer choice C.
27 B	Paragraph 2 introduces Henry's argument that the British are treating the Americans unfairly. Henry states, "I consider it as nothing less than a question of freedom or slavery," implying that he believes that the Americans are treated like slaves, answer choice B.
28 C	The best evidence for the comparison between the Americans and slaves can be found in lines 12-14, where Henry states, " For my own part, I consider it as nothing less than a question of freedom or slavery," comparing the Americans to slaves, answer choice C.
29 A	Henry describes that the illusions of hope allow the people to "shut our eyes against a painful truth." This means that the illusions of hope do not exist in reality, and are therefore a fantasy, answer choice A.
30 C	Henry gives the lamp human-like qualities by comparing it to a guide of experience. The lamp is an inanimate object, but is given qualities of a living organism in this sentence, also known as personification, answer choice C.
31 D	Henry asks the questions "Are fleets and armies necessary to a work of love and reconciliation?" and "Have we shown ourselves so unwilling to be reconciled that force must be called in to win back our love?" in order to make the audience question the motives of the British troops who have arrived in the American land, answer choice D.
32 C	Patrick Henry states that "These are the implements of war and subjugation," in reference to the questions that he posed in paragraph 5. This means that Henry considers the tactic of the British to be an act of war, answer choice C.
33 B	Henry uses this speech to show that the British cannot be bargained with, and that the British acts of war have proven to the Americans that they mean to enforce martial law, answer choice B.
34 A	The passage states that an advantage of Stem cells is that they can "differentiate into almost all types of bodily tissue." This means that the stem cell has a lot of properties that allow it to change into different types of tissue, answer choice A.

35 B	The passage states that the blastocyst "changes into an embryo" and is "a group of human cells that have not differentiated into anything yet." This outlines the role of a blastocyst as a lump of cells in the stage before turning into a human embryo, answer choice B.
36 D	The passage states that "embryonic stem cells can treat a wider range of diseases than adult stem cells," making answer choice D one of the reasons that embryonic stem cells are more useful than adult stem cells.
37 C	The author uses the word controversial to describe the argument on stem cells. An argument implies that there are two sides with conflicting or controversial ideas, answer choice C.
38 A	The passage states in lines 70-72 "Adult stem cell research will prosper if it gets the money currently going to embryonic stem cells, the pro-life supporters point out." This means that pro-life supporters believe that scientists should research adult stem cells, rather than embryonic stem cells, answer choice A.
39 C	The author appears to be addressing a public audience, as he or she does not specifically target a certain group of people. The author lists out arguments and speaks in a tone meant for a public audience, answer choice C.
40 A	The diagram shows that a majority of Republicans, 60%, are for stem cell research. This correlates to the argument of Excerpt 1, answer choice A.
41 A	The main argument of excerpt 1 is in support of stem cell research, while the main argument of excerpt 2 is against stem cell research. This means that the primary argument of excerpt 2 is challenged by excerpt 1, answer choice A.
42 B	The debate between the two excerpts is an ethical debate as it involves the usage of embryonic stem cells. Additionally, excerpt 1 states that "the benefits of stem cell research outweigh the ethical problem of destroying embryonic life," supporting the fact that the debate is over ethics, answer choice B.

PRACTICE TEST 3 - ANSWERS- WRITING AND LANGUAGE TEST

#	Explanation
1 D	To indicate possession of the birthplace, an apostrophe must be used with the word "ones." This means that the correct choice is "one's," answer choice D.
2 D	This sentence is written in the past tense. The current word, "counted," does not correctly match the tense of the sentence. To correct this, the word "count" must be used, answer choice D.
3 B	The sentence is asking a question, as shown by the words "Or is it the place..." This means that the sentence must end with a question mark, answer choice B.
4 D	To improve the flow of this sentence, it must be condensed. The words music, sounds, and tones all have similar meanings. Therefore only one of these words needs to be included in the list, answer choice D.
5 A	The phrase "the greatest anti-patriot of our time" is set off from the rest of the sentence. This means that it should be bounded by commas. Since the phrase already has commas before and after it, the sentence does not need further revision.
6 C	When introducing a list, there must be a comma before the word "and." This means that the sentence should say "arrogance, and egotism," answer choice C.
7 C	This additional statement presents the author's opinion, and does not have anything to do with the main idea of patriotism, answer choice C.
8 B	The word "pressing" indicates a sense of urgency to gain a greater army and navy. This means that pressing is the best replacement for the word "bargaining," answer choice B.
9 B	Sentence 3 introduces the meaning of the word "toys" as it is used in this passage. Sentence 1 discusses further on this topic. This means that sentence 3 should be placed before sentence 1, answer choice B.
10 C	Remember that proper nouns must always be capitalized. This means that the underlined words should be replaced with "San Francisco," answer choice C. No other punctuation is needed to revise the sentence.
11 B	The sentence is describing the rain forests of the world, meaning that the underlined word must show a form of possession. This means that "worlds" must be changed to "world's," answer choice B.
12 C	To adhere to correct English grammar, there must be a comma between a city and its country. This means that there should be a comma separating Moravia and Costa Rica, answer choice C.
13 D	The sentence does not appear to be a question, but rather appears to be a declarative sentence. The sentence describes some statistics about the world's rain forests and has a

	serious tone. This means that the sentence should end with a period, answer choice D.
14 D	The main idea of this paragraph is that rain forests allow vegetation to grow easily. Sentence 4 provides an opinion that does not relate to the main idea of the paragraph. This means that it should be removed to improve cohesion, answer choice D.
15 B	Jukofsky is positively describing the rainforest in this paragraph. The final two sentences of the paragraph indicate that the trees are very tall and can be seen above a person walking in the forest. This means that a better word to describe these trees is "tall," answer choice B.
16 C	This sentence is written in the present tense, describing medicine that is currently in usage. This means that the best tense for the word "growed" is one in the present, or "grow," answer choice C.
17 A	The phrase "As the destruction continues" is a dependent clause. This means that there needs to be a comma separating it from the rest of the sentence to improve the overall flow, answer choice A.
18 A	The main idea of this paragraph is that the cause of deforestation is the high amount of people who rely on its resources. At this point in the paragraph, a statistic about the amount of rainforest land used by families helps improve the clarity of the passage, answer choice A.
19 C	The best way to combine these two sentences is with a comma. Since the second sentence starts the word "and," a comma provides the best connection in between, answer choice C.
20 D	The underlined word needs to be converted into a proper contraction. This is the combination of the words "does" and "not." The corresponding contraction is "doesn't," answer choice D.
21 C	The subject of the sentence is the speaker, and therefore singular. To indicate that the speaker possesses her own rights, an apostrophe must be used after the word citizen. This means that the correct replacement is "citizen's," answer choice C.
22 C	When introducing a list of items, there needs to always be a comma before the word "and." This is only evident in answer choice C.
23 B	The following sentence discusses the formation of the Union. This means that a better replacement for the word "thought" is "created," answer choice B.
24 D	Violation, offense, and misconduct have similar definitions. This means that it is best to select only one of the three words to condense the sentence, answer choice D.
25 B	This statement shows that the future liberty of women is affected, which relates to the main idea of the passage. For this reason, the sentence should be included in the passage, answer choice B.
26 D	The speaker states in the beginning of the sentence, "the only question..." This means that the underlined phrase should end with a question mark, answer choice D.

27 A	The phrase "where the rich govern the poor" is a definition of the previously mentioned oligarchy. This means that it is best set aside from the rest of the sentence using a comma, answer choice A.
28 D	The word in the sentence, "patriatchy" is misspelled. The correct spelling is "patriarchy," answer choice D.
29 C	This sentence is a list of items written in the present tense. The corresponding verb in the present tense is "carries," answer choice C.
30 D	Paragraph 5 starts off with the statement, "The only question left..." meaning it is a concluding paragraph. The final sentence of paragraph 5 is also a conclusive statement. This means that this paragraph should be placed at the end of the passage, after paragraph 6, answer choice D.
31 A	The phrase "a region that today includes Syria, Lebanon, Israel, Jordan, and Iraq" is an interjection that needs to be set aside from the rest of the passage. This means that it should have a hyphen at the beginning and at the end, answer choice A.
32 D	Since the sentence does not just end after the quotation, there must be a comma placed at the end. This means that answer choice D is the correct revision.
33 C	To improve the flow of the sentence, the word "also" should appear at the beginning of the underlined statement. This means that answer choice C offers the best sentence flow out of all of the options. Rewritten: led by Johannes Krause, also a geneticist at the Max Planck Institute for the Science of Human History...
34 C	To indicate a change in idea, the best transition word to use in this case is "however." This means that answer choice C is the best revision for the split of these two sentences.
35 D	When introducing a list of items, a comma must always precede the word "and," answer choice D.
36 B	The best choice to indicate a greater sense of skepticism out of the answer choices is the word "intense." This shows that the amount of skepticism was very large, answer choice B.
37 A	To indicate possession in the first person, the word must end with an apostrophe and an "s". This means that the underlined phrase is grammatically correct, answer choice A.
38 B	Since the studies took place in the past, the underlined verb should be in the past tense as well. This means that the underlined word should be replaced with "used," answer choice B.
39 A	This additional sentence is necessary to describe the location that the scientists used to clean the surfaces of bone and soft tissue mentioned in the following sentence. For this reason, this additional sentence must be included in the passage, answer choice A.
40 C	This paragraph describes how scientists could extract genetic details from the mother's side of the family from the bones and teeth of Egyptian mummies. This is closest to the wording of answer choice C.

PRACTICE TEST 3 – ANSWERS – MATH TEST-No Calculator

#	Explanation
1 D	The equation can be rewritten as: $$3 + 2 = 3x - 2x$$ $$5 = x$$
2 C	If Bob drove 6 hours at 60 miles per hour, then he drove a total of $6 \cdot 60 = 360$ miles. If he still needed to drive 120 more miles, then his destination was $360 + 120 = 480$ miles away.
3 C	The bank account starts off with \$100. After 1 year it will have $100 \cdot 1.2 = \$120$. After 2 years it will have $100 \cdot 1.2 \cdot 1.2 = 100 \cdot 1.44 = \$144$.
4 A	This inequality can be rewritten as $$3d < 4$$ $$d < \frac{4}{3}$$ The only answer choice that is less than $\frac{4}{3}$ is answer choice A.
5 C	Car A can be modeled by the linear model $50h + 300$. Car B can be modeled by the linear model $60h$. Setting these two expressions equal to each other gives: $$50h + 300 = 60h$$ $$300 = 10h$$ $$h = 30$$ This means that after 30 hours, Car B will meet up with Car A.
6 B	In this situation, the slope is 7 as it is the rate of increase, and the y-intercept is 120, as it is the starting weight. This means that $w = 7y + 120$. This is the same as the equation given in answer choice B.
7 B	Two points on the graph are $(2,4)$ and $(1,2)$. The slope can be calculated using: $$\frac{4 - 2}{2 - 1} = \frac{2}{1} = 2$$
8 B	The velocity of the plane at 4 minutes is 8 meters per second. At 3 minutes the velocity of the plane is 6 meters per second. The difference between these two velocities is 2 meters per second.

9 C	The reservoir gained 1000 gallons in 2008, 2010, 2012, 2014, and 2016. This is a total increase of 5000 gallons in this time. The reservoir lost 500 gallons in 2009, 2011, 2013, and 2015. This is a total loss of 2000 gallons. 5000-2000=3000 gallons of water gained from 2008-2016.
10 C	Since the submarine is 1 mile beneath the Earth's surface, it is -1 mile from the Earth. This means that the absolute difference is $6 - (-1) = 7$ miles.
11 0	Multiplying the first equation by a factor of 2 gives: $$10x + 12y = 14$$ $$10x + 12y = 8$$ Since the coefficient values for the equations are the same, but the constant values are different, the two lines are parallel. This means that there are zero possible solutions for the system.
12 7	A ratio can be multiplied by a number to get equivalent ratio. In this case, if the team wins 2 more games the win-loss ratio will be 5:4, which is not what we are looking for. If the team wins 7 more games, the win-loss ratio will be 10:4, which is the same as 5:2.
13 2	The inequality can be rewritten as $$5x + 3 < 2x - 4 + 15$$ $$5x - 2x < -4 + 15 - 3$$ $$3x < 8$$ $$x < \frac{8}{3}$$ $$x < 2\frac{2}{3}$$ This means that the only positive integer solutions for x are 1 and 2.

#	Explanation
1 B	$$3^{-x} = 9$$ $$\frac{1}{3^x} = 9$$ $$3^x = \frac{1}{9}$$ $$x = -2$$
2 A	$$3(x + 2) = 3y$$ $$3x + 6 = 3y$$ $$x + 2 = y$$
3 B	Let x represent the total salary that Emily. $$0.35x = 300$$ $$x = \frac{300}{0.35} = \$857.14$$
4 D	The difference for ages 0-20 is 1000. The difference for ages 21-40 is 1000. The difference for ages 41-65 is 2000. The difference for ages 65+ is 3000, which is the greatest difference.
5 C	The population of 21-40 year olds is 6000+7000=13,000. The population of 0-20 year olds is 5000+6000=11,000. The difference between these two values is 2,000.
6 D	There are 3 paths from Tim's house to the library, and 5 from the library to the school. This means that there are $3 \cdot 5 = 15$ total pathways from his house to the school.
7 A	$$F = k \cdot \frac{q_1 \cdot q_2}{r^2}$$ $$r^2 = \frac{k \cdot q_1 \cdot q_2}{F}$$ $$r = \sqrt{\frac{k \cdot q_1 \cdot q_2}{F}}$$
8 C	The table shows that the values of $f(x)$ increase by the same amount for each value of x. This means that the table shows a linear relationship. Two points used to calculate the equation of the line are: (2,3) and (4,7):

$$\frac{7-3}{4-2} = \frac{4}{2} = 2$$

This means that $y = 2x + b$. We can use a data point to solve for the y-intercept:

$$3 = 2(2) + b$$
$$b = -1$$

The final equation is :

$$f(x) = 2x - 1$$

Plugging in 13 gives:

$$f(13) = 2 \cdot 13 - 1 = 26 - 1 = 25$$

9 C	John works at a rate of $\frac{1}{4}$ lawns per hour. Jeffrey works at a rate of $\frac{1}{7}$ lawns per hour. Therefore: $$\frac{1}{4} + \frac{1}{7} = \frac{11}{28} \; lawns \; per \; hour$$ Taking the reciprocal of this gives $\frac{28}{11} \; hours \; per \; lawn$.
10 B	The data points in the scatterplot show an exponential trend, as the distance between the points on the y-axis is increasing rapidly. This means that the line of best fit is exponential. 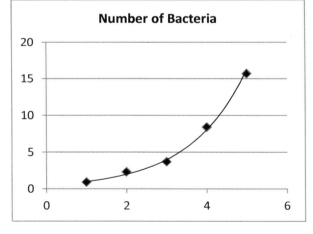
11 C	Since the line of best fit is exponential, the equation must be in the form $n = k^t$, where k is a constant. This means that the correct answer is C, $n = 2^t$.
12 A	$$\lvert 3x - 5 \rvert < 23$$ $$-23 < 3x - 5 < 23$$

$$-18 < 3x < 28$$

$$-6 < x < \frac{28}{3}$$

The only answer choice between these values is answer choice A, 0.

13 D	When the function is shifted down, the number 37 is subtracted from the constant value. This means that the new function is: $$f(x) = (x - 2)^2 + 6 - 37$$ $$f(x) = (x - 2)^2 - 31$$
14 D	Let x represent the number of cows in the farm, and let y represent the number of chickens. This scenario can be modeled using the following inequalities: $$x + y > 25$$ $$4x + 2y < 100$$ Answer choices B and C do not satisfy the first inequality. For answer choice A, $4 \cdot 30 + 2 \cdot 10 = 120 + 20 = 140$, which is not less than 100. This means that answer choice D is the correct answer.

15 D | We can begin filling in the missing information in the table one at a time:

	Soccer	Football	Total
Boys	10	20	
Girls		5	
Total		25	80

	Soccer	Football	Total
Boys	10	20	
Girls		5	
Total		25	80

	Soccer	Football	Total
Boys	10	20	30
Girls		5	
Total		25	80

	Soccer	Football	Total
Boys	10	20	30
Girls		5	50
Total		25	80

This means that a total of 50 girls were surveyed.

16 B	From filling the table out completely, there are 30 boys surveyed totally. Out of these 30, 20 of them have football as their favorite sport. This means $\frac{20}{30} = \frac{2}{3}$ of the boys chose football as their favorite sport.
17 D	From filling out the table completely, there are 45 girls who like soccer, and 20 boys who like football. This means that the ratio is $45:20$, which can be simplified to $9:4$.
18 B	The formulas given are $F = ma$ and $a = \frac{v}{t}$. We can use substitution to rewrite the first formula: $$F = m \cdot \left(\frac{v}{t}\right)$$ In the problem, we are given that $m = 2kg$, $v = 5\ meters\ per\ second$, and $t = 10\ seconds$. Plugging these into the equation above gives: $$F = 2 \cdot \left(\frac{5}{10}\right) = 1N$$
19 A	$$f\big(g(x)\big) = f(2x + 5)$$ $$f(2x + 5) = 3 \cdot (2x + 5)^2$$
20 C	The equations can be set equal to each other as follows: $$x^4 = 16$$ $$x = \sqrt[4]{16}$$ $$x = \pm 2$$ $$x = -2, 2$$ There are two solutions for the system. Additionally, the two functions can be graphed and the intersections can be seen visually below:

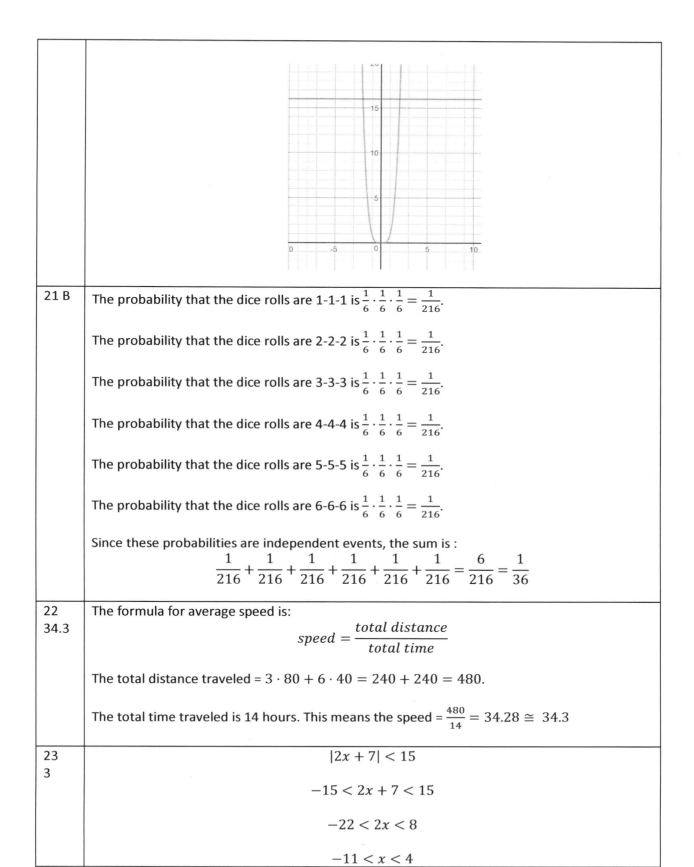

21 B	The probability that the dice rolls are 1-1-1 is $\frac{1}{6} \cdot \frac{1}{6} \cdot \frac{1}{6} = \frac{1}{216}$.
	The probability that the dice rolls are 2-2-2 is $\frac{1}{6} \cdot \frac{1}{6} \cdot \frac{1}{6} = \frac{1}{216}$.
	The probability that the dice rolls are 3-3-3 is $\frac{1}{6} \cdot \frac{1}{6} \cdot \frac{1}{6} = \frac{1}{216}$.
	The probability that the dice rolls are 4-4-4 is $\frac{1}{6} \cdot \frac{1}{6} \cdot \frac{1}{6} = \frac{1}{216}$.
	The probability that the dice rolls are 5-5-5 is $\frac{1}{6} \cdot \frac{1}{6} \cdot \frac{1}{6} = \frac{1}{216}$.
	The probability that the dice rolls are 6-6-6 is $\frac{1}{6} \cdot \frac{1}{6} \cdot \frac{1}{6} = \frac{1}{216}$.
	Since these probabilities are independent events, the sum is : $$\frac{1}{216} + \frac{1}{216} + \frac{1}{216} + \frac{1}{216} + \frac{1}{216} + \frac{1}{216} = \frac{6}{216} = \frac{1}{36}$$
22 34.3	The formula for average speed is: $$speed = \frac{total\ distance}{total\ time}$$ The total distance traveled $= 3 \cdot 80 + 6 \cdot 40 = 240 + 240 = 480$. The total time traveled is 14 hours. This means the speed $= \frac{480}{14} = 34.28 \cong 34.3$
23 3	$$|2x + 7| < 15$$ $$-15 < 2x + 7 < 15$$ $$-22 < 2x < 8$$ $$-11 < x < 4$$

	The positive integer solutions are 1, 2, and 3, for a total of 3 positive integer solutions.
24 34	The best way to approach this problem is to guess and check the values of $z \cdot k$. $$-17 \cdot 5 = -85$$ $$5 \cdot 3 = 15$$ $$-17 \cdot -2 = 34$$ After guessing and checking some values, 34 can be calculated to be the largest values of $z \cdot k$.
25 22	$$\sqrt{x + 2} = 2x + 3$$ $$x + 2 = (2x + 3)^2$$ $$x + 2 = 4x^2 + 12x + 9$$ $$0 = 4x^2 + 11x + 7$$ Therefore, $a = 4, b = 11, and\ c = 7$. The sum $4 + 11 + 7 = 22$

Acknowledgements

Achebe, Chinua. "Things Fall Apart." *L. Adam Mekler*, l-adam-mekler.com/things-fall-apart.pdf.

"Adding Ice to Medics' Kits Could Help Patients Survive Blood Loss." *Science News for Students*, www.sciencenewsforstudents.org/article/adding-ice-medics-kits-could-help-patients-survive-blood-loss.

"Arguments Against Stem Cell Research." *Odec - Online Digital Education Connection*, www.odec.ca/projects/2008/hess8s2/argumentsagainst.html.

"BBC - Higher Bitesize Geography - Atmosphere : Revision, Page2." *BBC - Home*, www.bbc.co.uk/bitesize/higher/geography/physical/atmosphere/revision/2/.

"BBC NEWS | Science/Nature | Methane Rise Points to Wetlands." *Home - BBC News*, news.bbc.co.uk/1/hi/sci/tech/7408808.stm.

"Brains Encode Faces Piece by Piece." *Science News*, www.sciencenews.org/article/brains-encode-faces-piece-piece?tgt=nr.

"A Brief Overview of the American Civil War." *Civil War Trust*, www.civilwar.org/learn/articles/brief-overview-american-civil-war.

Burnett, Frances H. "The Secret Garden." *Gutenberg*, Project Gutenberg, www.gutenberg.org/files/113/113-h/113-h.htm.

"Can These Plastic-Eating Wax Worms Help Reduce Our Trash? Kids News Article." *DOGOnews*, www.dogonews.com/2017/5/25/can-these-plastic-eating-wax-worms-help-reduce-our-trash.

"Climate Change: Vital Signs of the Planet: Keeping an Eye on Food Supply." *Climate Change: Vital Signs of the Planet*, climate.nasa.gov/news/2582/keeping-an-eye-on-food-supply/.

"Emma Goldman Speech - What Is Patriotism." *Famous Speeches and Speech Topics*,

   www.famous-speeches-and-speech-topics.info/famous-speeches/emma-goldman-speech-

   what-is-patriotism.htm.

""Enemies from Within": Senator Joseph R. McCarthy's Accusations of Disloyalty." *History*

   Matters: The U.S. Survey Course on the Web, historymatters.gmu.edu/d/6456.

""Enemies from Within": Senator Joseph R. McCarthy's Accusations of Disloyalty." *History*

   Matters: The U.S. Survey Course on the Web, historymatters.gmu.edu/d/6456.

"Global Warming : Feature Articles." *NASA Earth Observatory : Home*,

   earthobservatory.nasa.gov/Features/GlobalWarming/page2.php.

Hesse, Hermann. "Siddhartha." *Gutenberg*, Project Gutenberg,

   www.gutenberg.org/files/2500/2500-h/2500-h.htm.

"How the Galapagos Cormorant Forgot How to Fly." *Popular Science*,

   www.popsci.com/galapagos-cormorant-flightless#page-2.

"Indira Gandhi: What Educated Women Can Do." *SoJust: Primary Source History of Social*

   Justice and Human Rights in Speeches & Songs,

   www.sojust.net/speeches/indira_gandhi_educated.html.

"The Industrial Revolution: Past and Future." *Federal Reserve Bank of Minneapolis*,

   minneapolisfed.org/publications/the-region/the-industrial-revolution-past-and-future.

"John F. Kennedy: Inaugural Address." *The American Presidency Project*,

   www.presidency.ucsb.edu/ws/?pid=8032.

"Making the World "Safe for Democracy": Woodrow Wilson Asks for War." *History Matters:*

   The U.S. Survey Course on the Web, historymatters.gmu.edu/d/4943/.

"Patrick Henry: The War Inevitable." *SoJust: Primary Source History of Social Justice and Human Rights in Speeches & Songs*, www.sojust.net/speeches/patrickhenry_war.html.

"The PSAT 8/9 – The College Board." *SAT Suite of Assessments*, collegereadiness.collegeboard.org/psat-8-9.

"The Quit India Speeches | Famous Speeches by Mahatma Gandhi." *WELCOME TO MAHATMA GANDHI ONE SPOT COMPLETE INFORMATION WEBSITE*, www.mkgandhi.org/speeches/qui.htm.

"Sapping Attention: The Age of Capital–." *Sapping Attention*, sappingattention.blogspot.com/2010/12/age-of-capital.html

"Scholastic News: Rain Forest." *Scholastic Publishes Literacy Resources and Children's Books for Kids of All Ages*, teacher.scholastic.com/scholasticnews/indepth/rainforest/rainforest.asp.

"Speech on Communism in Elberfeld. Moses Hess. 1845." *Marxists Internet Archive*, www.marxists.org/archive/hess/1845/elberfeld-speech.htm.

"Surprising Find: Ancient Mummy DNA Sequenced in First." *Live Science*, www.livescience.com/59410-ancient-egyptian-mummy-dna-sequenced.html.

"Susan B. Anthony: Historic Multicultural Speeches: On Women's Right to Vote." *SoJust: Primary Source History of Social Justice and Human Rights in Speeches & Songs*, www.sojust.net/speeches/susananthony.html.

"Third Black-Hole Merger Proves (Yet Again) That Einstein Was Right - History in the Headlines." *HISTORY.com*, www.history.com/news/third-black-hole-merger-proves-yet-again-that-einstein-was-right.

"Townipproject - Stem Cell Research." *Townipproject - Home*,

ownipproject.wikispaces.com/Stem+Cell+Research.

"Treaty of Versailles, 1919." *United States Holocaust Memorial Museum*,

www.ushmm.org/wlc/en/article.php?ModuleId=10005425.

"US History: World War I Fast Facts Homework Questions." *US History*,

lalalatteush.blogspot.com/2015/03/world-war-i-fast-facts-homework.html.

"The War and the Intellectuals: Randolph Bourne Vents His Animus Against War." *History

Matters: The U.S. Survey Course on the Web*, historymatters.gmu.edu/d/4941.

"Winston Churchill Speech - Their Finest Hour." *Famous Speeches and Speech Topics*,

www.famous-speeches-and-speech-topics.info/famous-speeches/winston-churchill-

speech-their-finest-hour.htm.

"The Zika Epidemic Began Long Before Anyone Noticed." *Science News*,

www.sciencenews.org/article/zika-epidemic-began-long-anyone-noticed?tgt=nr.

GRID IN RESPONSE DIRECTIONS

- Solve the GRID-IN questions, and then enter your answer in the grids provided.
- Write your answer in the boxes at the top of the columns.
- Grid-in your answer in the columns below the boxes. Only mark one circle per column.
- All answers are positive real numbers.
- For a problem with multiple answers, grid in only one answer.
- Mixed numbers such as $2\frac{1}{2}$ must be gridded in as $\frac{5}{2}$ or 2.5. Do not grid in as 21/2.
- Decimal answers must be either rounded or truncated to fill up the entire grid.

Answer: $\frac{4}{13}$ Answer: 5.7   Answer: 123

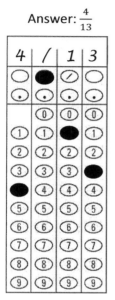
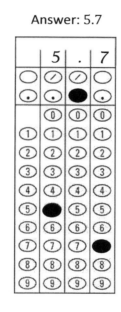
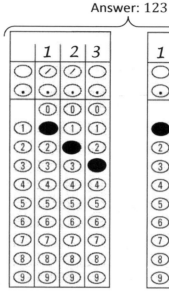
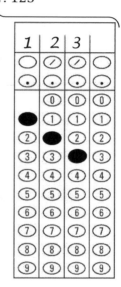

Answer: $\frac{5}{11} = 0.45454545\ldots$

ANSWER SHEET * PRACTICE TEST 1
SECTION 1: READING TEST

1. Ⓐ Ⓑ Ⓒ Ⓓ
2. Ⓐ Ⓑ Ⓒ Ⓓ
3. Ⓐ Ⓑ Ⓒ Ⓓ
4. Ⓐ Ⓑ Ⓒ Ⓓ
5. Ⓐ Ⓑ Ⓒ Ⓓ
6. Ⓐ Ⓑ Ⓒ Ⓓ
7. Ⓐ Ⓑ Ⓒ Ⓓ
8. Ⓐ Ⓑ Ⓒ Ⓓ
9. Ⓐ Ⓑ Ⓒ Ⓓ
10. Ⓐ Ⓑ Ⓒ Ⓓ
11. Ⓐ Ⓑ Ⓒ Ⓓ
12. Ⓐ Ⓑ Ⓒ Ⓓ
13. Ⓐ Ⓑ Ⓒ Ⓓ
14. Ⓐ Ⓑ Ⓒ Ⓓ

15. Ⓐ Ⓑ Ⓒ Ⓓ
16. Ⓐ Ⓑ Ⓒ Ⓓ
17. Ⓐ Ⓑ Ⓒ Ⓓ
18. Ⓐ Ⓑ Ⓒ Ⓓ
19. Ⓐ Ⓑ Ⓒ Ⓓ
20. Ⓐ Ⓑ Ⓒ Ⓓ
21. Ⓐ Ⓑ Ⓒ Ⓓ
22. Ⓐ Ⓑ Ⓒ Ⓓ
23. Ⓐ Ⓑ Ⓒ Ⓓ
24. Ⓐ Ⓑ Ⓒ Ⓓ
25. Ⓐ Ⓑ Ⓒ Ⓓ
26. Ⓐ Ⓑ Ⓒ Ⓓ
27. Ⓐ Ⓑ Ⓒ Ⓓ
28. Ⓐ Ⓑ Ⓒ Ⓓ

29. Ⓐ Ⓑ Ⓒ Ⓓ
30. Ⓐ Ⓑ Ⓒ Ⓓ
31. Ⓐ Ⓑ Ⓒ Ⓓ
32. Ⓐ Ⓑ Ⓒ Ⓓ
33. Ⓐ Ⓑ Ⓒ Ⓓ
34. Ⓐ Ⓑ Ⓒ Ⓓ
35. Ⓐ Ⓑ Ⓒ Ⓓ
36. Ⓐ Ⓑ Ⓒ Ⓓ
37. Ⓐ Ⓑ Ⓒ Ⓓ
38. Ⓐ Ⓑ Ⓒ Ⓓ
39. Ⓐ Ⓑ Ⓒ Ⓓ
40. Ⓐ Ⓑ Ⓒ Ⓓ
41. Ⓐ Ⓑ Ⓒ Ⓓ
42. Ⓐ Ⓑ Ⓒ Ⓓ

ANSWER SHEET * PRACTICE TEST 1
SECTION 2: WRITING & LANGUAGE TEST

1. Ⓐ Ⓑ Ⓒ Ⓓ
2. Ⓐ Ⓑ Ⓒ Ⓓ
3. Ⓐ Ⓑ Ⓒ Ⓓ
4. Ⓐ Ⓑ Ⓒ Ⓓ
5. Ⓐ Ⓑ Ⓒ Ⓓ
6. Ⓐ Ⓑ Ⓒ Ⓓ
7. Ⓐ Ⓑ Ⓒ Ⓓ
8. Ⓐ Ⓑ Ⓒ Ⓓ
9. Ⓐ Ⓑ Ⓒ Ⓓ
10. Ⓐ Ⓑ Ⓒ Ⓓ
11. Ⓐ Ⓑ Ⓒ Ⓓ
12. Ⓐ Ⓑ Ⓒ Ⓓ
13. Ⓐ Ⓑ Ⓒ Ⓓ
14. Ⓐ Ⓑ Ⓒ Ⓓ

15. Ⓐ Ⓑ Ⓒ Ⓓ
16. Ⓐ Ⓑ Ⓒ Ⓓ
17. Ⓐ Ⓑ Ⓒ Ⓓ
18. Ⓐ Ⓑ Ⓒ Ⓓ
19. Ⓐ Ⓑ Ⓒ Ⓓ
20. Ⓐ Ⓑ Ⓒ Ⓓ
21. Ⓐ Ⓑ Ⓒ Ⓓ
22. Ⓐ Ⓑ Ⓒ Ⓓ
23. Ⓐ Ⓑ Ⓒ Ⓓ
24. Ⓐ Ⓑ Ⓒ Ⓓ
25. Ⓐ Ⓑ Ⓒ Ⓓ
26. Ⓐ Ⓑ Ⓒ Ⓓ
27. Ⓐ Ⓑ Ⓒ Ⓓ
28. Ⓐ Ⓑ Ⓒ Ⓓ

29. Ⓐ Ⓑ Ⓒ Ⓓ
30. Ⓐ Ⓑ Ⓒ Ⓓ
31. Ⓐ Ⓑ Ⓒ Ⓓ
32. Ⓐ Ⓑ Ⓒ Ⓓ
33. Ⓐ Ⓑ Ⓒ Ⓓ
34. Ⓐ Ⓑ Ⓒ Ⓓ
35. Ⓐ Ⓑ Ⓒ Ⓓ
36. Ⓐ Ⓑ Ⓒ Ⓓ
37. Ⓐ Ⓑ Ⓒ Ⓓ
38. Ⓐ Ⓑ Ⓒ Ⓓ
39. Ⓐ Ⓑ Ⓒ Ⓓ
40. Ⓐ Ⓑ Ⓒ Ⓓ

ANSWER SHEET * PRACTICE TEST 1

SECTION 3: MATH-NO CALCULATOR

1. Ⓐ Ⓑ Ⓒ Ⓓ
2. Ⓐ Ⓑ Ⓒ Ⓓ
3. Ⓐ Ⓑ Ⓒ Ⓓ
4. Ⓐ Ⓑ Ⓒ Ⓓ
5. Ⓐ Ⓑ Ⓒ Ⓓ
6. Ⓐ Ⓑ Ⓒ Ⓓ
7. Ⓐ Ⓑ Ⓒ Ⓓ
8. Ⓐ Ⓑ Ⓒ Ⓓ
9. Ⓐ Ⓑ Ⓒ Ⓓ
10. Ⓐ Ⓑ Ⓒ Ⓓ

11.

12.

13.

ANSWER SHEET * PRACTICE TEST 1

SECTION 4: MATH-CALCULATOR

1. Ⓐ Ⓑ Ⓒ Ⓓ
2. Ⓐ Ⓑ Ⓒ Ⓓ
3. Ⓐ Ⓑ Ⓒ Ⓓ
4. Ⓐ Ⓑ Ⓒ Ⓓ
5. Ⓐ Ⓑ Ⓒ Ⓓ
6. Ⓐ Ⓑ Ⓒ Ⓓ
7. Ⓐ Ⓑ Ⓒ Ⓓ

8. Ⓐ Ⓑ Ⓒ Ⓓ
9. Ⓐ Ⓑ Ⓒ Ⓓ
10. Ⓐ Ⓑ Ⓒ Ⓓ
11. Ⓐ Ⓑ Ⓒ Ⓓ
12. Ⓐ Ⓑ Ⓒ Ⓓ
13. Ⓐ Ⓑ Ⓒ Ⓓ
14. Ⓐ Ⓑ Ⓒ Ⓓ

15. Ⓐ Ⓑ Ⓒ Ⓓ
16. Ⓐ Ⓑ Ⓒ Ⓓ
17. Ⓐ Ⓑ Ⓒ Ⓓ
18. Ⓐ Ⓑ Ⓒ Ⓓ
19. Ⓐ Ⓑ Ⓒ Ⓓ
20. Ⓐ Ⓑ Ⓒ Ⓓ
21. Ⓐ Ⓑ Ⓒ Ⓓ

22.

23.

24.

25.

ANSWER SHEET * PRACTICE TEST 2
SECTION 1: READING TEST

1. Ⓐ Ⓑ Ⓒ Ⓓ
2. Ⓐ Ⓑ Ⓒ Ⓓ
3. Ⓐ Ⓑ Ⓒ Ⓓ
4. Ⓐ Ⓑ Ⓒ Ⓓ
5. Ⓐ Ⓑ Ⓒ Ⓓ
6. Ⓐ Ⓑ Ⓒ Ⓓ
7. Ⓐ Ⓑ Ⓒ Ⓓ
8. Ⓐ Ⓑ Ⓒ Ⓓ
9. Ⓐ Ⓑ Ⓒ Ⓓ
10. Ⓐ Ⓑ Ⓒ Ⓓ
11. Ⓐ Ⓑ Ⓒ Ⓓ
12. Ⓐ Ⓑ Ⓒ Ⓓ
13. Ⓐ Ⓑ Ⓒ Ⓓ
14. Ⓐ Ⓑ Ⓒ Ⓓ

15. Ⓐ Ⓑ Ⓒ Ⓓ
16. Ⓐ Ⓑ Ⓒ Ⓓ
17. Ⓐ Ⓑ Ⓒ Ⓓ
18. Ⓐ Ⓑ Ⓒ Ⓓ
19. Ⓐ Ⓑ Ⓒ Ⓓ
20. Ⓐ Ⓑ Ⓒ Ⓓ
21. Ⓐ Ⓑ Ⓒ Ⓓ
22. Ⓐ Ⓑ Ⓒ Ⓓ
23. Ⓐ Ⓑ Ⓒ Ⓓ
24. Ⓐ Ⓑ Ⓒ Ⓓ
25. Ⓐ Ⓑ Ⓒ Ⓓ
26. Ⓐ Ⓑ Ⓒ Ⓓ
27. Ⓐ Ⓑ Ⓒ Ⓓ
28. Ⓐ Ⓑ Ⓒ Ⓓ

29. Ⓐ Ⓑ Ⓒ Ⓓ
30. Ⓐ Ⓑ Ⓒ Ⓓ
31. Ⓐ Ⓑ Ⓒ Ⓓ
32. Ⓐ Ⓑ Ⓒ Ⓓ
33. Ⓐ Ⓑ Ⓒ Ⓓ
34. Ⓐ Ⓑ Ⓒ Ⓓ
35. Ⓐ Ⓑ Ⓒ Ⓓ
36. Ⓐ Ⓑ Ⓒ Ⓓ
37. Ⓐ Ⓑ Ⓒ Ⓓ
38. Ⓐ Ⓑ Ⓒ Ⓓ
39. Ⓐ Ⓑ Ⓒ Ⓓ
40. Ⓐ Ⓑ Ⓒ Ⓓ
41. Ⓐ Ⓑ Ⓒ Ⓓ
42. Ⓐ Ⓑ Ⓒ Ⓓ

ANSWER SHEET * PRACTICE TEST 2
SECTION 2: WRITING & LANGUAGE TEST

1. Ⓐ Ⓑ Ⓒ Ⓓ
2. Ⓐ Ⓑ Ⓒ Ⓓ
3. Ⓐ Ⓑ Ⓒ Ⓓ
4. Ⓐ Ⓑ Ⓒ Ⓓ
5. Ⓐ Ⓑ Ⓒ Ⓓ
6. Ⓐ Ⓑ Ⓒ Ⓓ
7. Ⓐ Ⓑ Ⓒ Ⓓ
8. Ⓐ Ⓑ Ⓒ Ⓓ
9. Ⓐ Ⓑ Ⓒ Ⓓ
10. Ⓐ Ⓑ Ⓒ Ⓓ
11. Ⓐ Ⓑ Ⓒ Ⓓ
12. Ⓐ Ⓑ Ⓒ Ⓓ
13. Ⓐ Ⓑ Ⓒ Ⓓ
14. Ⓐ Ⓑ Ⓒ Ⓓ

15. Ⓐ Ⓑ Ⓒ Ⓓ
16. Ⓐ Ⓑ Ⓒ Ⓓ
17. Ⓐ Ⓑ Ⓒ Ⓓ
18. Ⓐ Ⓑ Ⓒ Ⓓ
19. Ⓐ Ⓑ Ⓒ Ⓓ
20. Ⓐ Ⓑ Ⓒ Ⓓ
21. Ⓐ Ⓑ Ⓒ Ⓓ
22. Ⓐ Ⓑ Ⓒ Ⓓ
23. Ⓐ Ⓑ Ⓒ Ⓓ
24. Ⓐ Ⓑ Ⓒ Ⓓ
25. Ⓐ Ⓑ Ⓒ Ⓓ
26. Ⓐ Ⓑ Ⓒ Ⓓ
27. Ⓐ Ⓑ Ⓒ Ⓓ
28. Ⓐ Ⓑ Ⓒ Ⓓ

29. Ⓐ Ⓑ Ⓒ Ⓓ
30. Ⓐ Ⓑ Ⓒ Ⓓ
31. Ⓐ Ⓑ Ⓒ Ⓓ
32. Ⓐ Ⓑ Ⓒ Ⓓ
33. Ⓐ Ⓑ Ⓒ Ⓓ
34. Ⓐ Ⓑ Ⓒ Ⓓ
35. Ⓐ Ⓑ Ⓒ Ⓓ
36. Ⓐ Ⓑ Ⓒ Ⓓ
37. Ⓐ Ⓑ Ⓒ Ⓓ
38. Ⓐ Ⓑ Ⓒ Ⓓ
39. Ⓐ Ⓑ Ⓒ Ⓓ
40. Ⓐ Ⓑ Ⓒ Ⓓ

ANSWER SHEET * PRACTICE TEST 2

SECTION 3: MATH-NO CALCULATOR

1. Ⓐ Ⓑ Ⓒ Ⓓ
2. Ⓐ Ⓑ Ⓒ Ⓓ
3. Ⓐ Ⓑ Ⓒ Ⓓ
4. Ⓐ Ⓑ Ⓒ Ⓓ
5. Ⓐ Ⓑ Ⓒ Ⓓ
6. Ⓐ Ⓑ Ⓒ Ⓓ
7. Ⓐ Ⓑ Ⓒ Ⓓ
8. Ⓐ Ⓑ Ⓒ Ⓓ
9. Ⓐ Ⓑ Ⓒ Ⓓ
10. Ⓐ Ⓑ Ⓒ Ⓓ

11.

12.

13.

SECTION 4: MATH-CALCULATOR

1. Ⓐ Ⓑ Ⓒ Ⓓ	8. Ⓐ Ⓑ Ⓒ Ⓓ	15. Ⓐ Ⓑ Ⓒ Ⓓ
2. Ⓐ Ⓑ Ⓒ Ⓓ	9. Ⓐ Ⓑ Ⓒ Ⓓ	16. Ⓐ Ⓑ Ⓒ Ⓓ
3. Ⓐ Ⓑ Ⓒ Ⓓ	10. Ⓐ Ⓑ Ⓒ Ⓓ	17. Ⓐ Ⓑ Ⓒ Ⓓ
4. Ⓐ Ⓑ Ⓒ Ⓓ	11. Ⓐ Ⓑ Ⓒ Ⓓ	18. Ⓐ Ⓑ Ⓒ Ⓓ
5. Ⓐ Ⓑ Ⓒ Ⓓ	12. Ⓐ Ⓑ Ⓒ Ⓓ	19. Ⓐ Ⓑ Ⓒ Ⓓ
6. Ⓐ Ⓑ Ⓒ Ⓓ	13. Ⓐ Ⓑ Ⓒ Ⓓ	20. Ⓐ Ⓑ Ⓒ Ⓓ
7. Ⓐ Ⓑ Ⓒ Ⓓ	14. Ⓐ Ⓑ Ⓒ Ⓓ	21. Ⓐ Ⓑ Ⓒ Ⓓ

22.

23.

24.

25.

ANSWER SHEET * PRACTICE TEST 3
SECTION 1: READING TEST

1. Ⓐ Ⓑ Ⓒ Ⓓ	15. Ⓐ Ⓑ Ⓒ Ⓓ	29. Ⓐ Ⓑ Ⓒ Ⓓ
2. Ⓐ Ⓑ Ⓒ Ⓓ	16. Ⓐ Ⓑ Ⓒ Ⓓ	30. Ⓐ Ⓑ Ⓒ Ⓓ
3. Ⓐ Ⓑ Ⓒ Ⓓ	17. Ⓐ Ⓑ Ⓒ Ⓓ	31. Ⓐ Ⓑ Ⓒ Ⓓ
4. Ⓐ Ⓑ Ⓒ Ⓓ	18. Ⓐ Ⓑ Ⓒ Ⓓ	32. Ⓐ Ⓑ Ⓒ Ⓓ
5. Ⓐ Ⓑ Ⓒ Ⓓ	19. Ⓐ Ⓑ Ⓒ Ⓓ	33. Ⓐ Ⓑ Ⓒ Ⓓ
6. Ⓐ Ⓑ Ⓒ Ⓓ	20. Ⓐ Ⓑ Ⓒ Ⓓ	34. Ⓐ Ⓑ Ⓒ Ⓓ
7. Ⓐ Ⓑ Ⓒ Ⓓ	21. Ⓐ Ⓑ Ⓒ Ⓓ	35. Ⓐ Ⓑ Ⓒ Ⓓ
8. Ⓐ Ⓑ Ⓒ Ⓓ	22. Ⓐ Ⓑ Ⓒ Ⓓ	36. Ⓐ Ⓑ Ⓒ Ⓓ
9. Ⓐ Ⓑ Ⓒ Ⓓ	23. Ⓐ Ⓑ Ⓒ Ⓓ	37. Ⓐ Ⓑ Ⓒ Ⓓ
10. Ⓐ Ⓑ Ⓒ Ⓓ	24. Ⓐ Ⓑ Ⓒ Ⓓ	38. Ⓐ Ⓑ Ⓒ Ⓓ
11. Ⓐ Ⓑ Ⓒ Ⓓ	25. Ⓐ Ⓑ Ⓒ Ⓓ	39. Ⓐ Ⓑ Ⓒ Ⓓ
12. Ⓐ Ⓑ Ⓒ Ⓓ	26. Ⓐ Ⓑ Ⓒ Ⓓ	40. Ⓐ Ⓑ Ⓒ Ⓓ
13. Ⓐ Ⓑ Ⓒ Ⓓ	27. Ⓐ Ⓑ Ⓒ Ⓓ	41. Ⓐ Ⓑ Ⓒ Ⓓ
14. Ⓐ Ⓑ Ⓒ Ⓓ	28. Ⓐ Ⓑ Ⓒ Ⓓ	42. Ⓐ Ⓑ Ⓒ Ⓓ

ANSWER SHEET * PRACTICE TEST 3
SECTION 2: WRITING & LANGUAGE TEST

1. Ⓐ Ⓑ Ⓒ Ⓓ	15. Ⓐ Ⓑ Ⓒ Ⓓ	29. Ⓐ Ⓑ Ⓒ Ⓓ
2. Ⓐ Ⓑ Ⓒ Ⓓ	16. Ⓐ Ⓑ Ⓒ Ⓓ	30. Ⓐ Ⓑ Ⓒ Ⓓ
3. Ⓐ Ⓑ Ⓒ Ⓓ	17. Ⓐ Ⓑ Ⓒ Ⓓ	31. Ⓐ Ⓑ Ⓒ Ⓓ
4. Ⓐ Ⓑ Ⓒ Ⓓ	18. Ⓐ Ⓑ Ⓒ Ⓓ	32. Ⓐ Ⓑ Ⓒ Ⓓ
5. Ⓐ Ⓑ Ⓒ Ⓓ	19. Ⓐ Ⓑ Ⓒ Ⓓ	33. Ⓐ Ⓑ Ⓒ Ⓓ
6. Ⓐ Ⓑ Ⓒ Ⓓ	20. Ⓐ Ⓑ Ⓒ Ⓓ	34. Ⓐ Ⓑ Ⓒ Ⓓ
7. Ⓐ Ⓑ Ⓒ Ⓓ	21. Ⓐ Ⓑ Ⓒ Ⓓ	35. Ⓐ Ⓑ Ⓒ Ⓓ
8. Ⓐ Ⓑ Ⓒ Ⓓ	22. Ⓐ Ⓑ Ⓒ Ⓓ	36. Ⓐ Ⓑ Ⓒ Ⓓ
9. Ⓐ Ⓑ Ⓒ Ⓓ	23. Ⓐ Ⓑ Ⓒ Ⓓ	37. Ⓐ Ⓑ Ⓒ Ⓓ
10. Ⓐ Ⓑ Ⓒ Ⓓ	24. Ⓐ Ⓑ Ⓒ Ⓓ	38. Ⓐ Ⓑ Ⓒ Ⓓ
11. Ⓐ Ⓑ Ⓒ Ⓓ	25. Ⓐ Ⓑ Ⓒ Ⓓ	39. Ⓐ Ⓑ Ⓒ Ⓓ
12. Ⓐ Ⓑ Ⓒ Ⓓ	26. Ⓐ Ⓑ Ⓒ Ⓓ	40. Ⓐ Ⓑ Ⓒ Ⓓ
13. Ⓐ Ⓑ Ⓒ Ⓓ	27. Ⓐ Ⓑ Ⓒ Ⓓ	
14. Ⓐ Ⓑ Ⓒ Ⓓ	28. Ⓐ Ⓑ Ⓒ Ⓓ	

ANSWER SHEET * PRACTICE TEST 3
SECTION 3: MATH-NO CALCULATOR

1. Ⓐ Ⓑ Ⓒ Ⓓ
2. Ⓐ Ⓑ Ⓒ Ⓓ
3. Ⓐ Ⓑ Ⓒ Ⓓ
4. Ⓐ Ⓑ Ⓒ Ⓓ
5. Ⓐ Ⓑ Ⓒ Ⓓ
6. Ⓐ Ⓑ Ⓒ Ⓓ
7. Ⓐ Ⓑ Ⓒ Ⓓ
8. Ⓐ Ⓑ Ⓒ Ⓓ
9. Ⓐ Ⓑ Ⓒ Ⓓ
10. Ⓐ Ⓑ Ⓒ Ⓓ

11.

12.

13.

ANSWER SHEET * PRACTICE TEST 3
SECTION 4: MATH-CALCULATOR

1. Ⓐ Ⓑ Ⓒ Ⓓ
2. Ⓐ Ⓑ Ⓒ Ⓓ
3. Ⓐ Ⓑ Ⓒ Ⓓ
4. Ⓐ Ⓑ Ⓒ Ⓓ
5. Ⓐ Ⓑ Ⓒ Ⓓ
6. Ⓐ Ⓑ Ⓒ Ⓓ
7. Ⓐ Ⓑ Ⓒ Ⓓ

8. Ⓐ Ⓑ Ⓒ Ⓓ
9. Ⓐ Ⓑ Ⓒ Ⓓ
10. Ⓐ Ⓑ Ⓒ Ⓓ
11. Ⓐ Ⓑ Ⓒ Ⓓ
12. Ⓐ Ⓑ Ⓒ Ⓓ
13. Ⓐ Ⓑ Ⓒ Ⓓ
14. Ⓐ Ⓑ Ⓒ Ⓓ

15. Ⓐ Ⓑ Ⓒ Ⓓ
16. Ⓐ Ⓑ Ⓒ Ⓓ
17. Ⓐ Ⓑ Ⓒ Ⓓ
18. Ⓐ Ⓑ Ⓒ Ⓓ
19. Ⓐ Ⓑ Ⓒ Ⓓ
20. Ⓐ Ⓑ Ⓒ Ⓓ
21. Ⓐ Ⓑ Ⓒ Ⓓ

22.

23.

24.

25.

SCORING SHEET : PRACTICE TEST 1

Test 1- Section 1 Reading		Test 1- Section 2 Writing and Language		Test 1- Section 3 Math No-Calculator		Test 1- Section 4 Math Calculator	
Q#	Answer	Q#	Answer	Q#	Answer	Q#	Answer
1	D	1	D	1	D	1	B
2	C	2	A	2	D	2	C
3	B	3	B	3	A	3	D
4	C	4	B	4	B	4	A
5	A	5	D	5	B	5	D
6	B	6	B	6	B	6	B
7	A	7	B	7	C	7	B
8	D	8	D	8	C	8	A
9	A	9	C	9	B	9	D
10	C	10	D	10	D	10	D
11	C	11	A	11	200	11	B
12	D	12	C	12	6	12	D
13	B	13	A	13	0	13	D
14	C	14	B	Correct:		14	D
15	D	15	D			15	B
16	C	16	B			16	B
17	A	17	A			17	A
18	A	18	C			18	C
19	C	19	C			19	A
20	C	20	B			20	C
21	B	21	D			21	A
22	A	22	D			22	80
23	D	23	A			23	10
24	A	24	B			24	1341
25	C	25	C			25	106
26	B	26	C			Correct:	
27	D	27	D				
28	B	28	A				
29	D	29	D				
30	B	30	A				
31	A	31	B				
32	A	32	D				
33	C	33	B				
34	A	34	C				
35	D	35	A				
36	D	36	B				
37	A	37	A				
38	B	38	C				
39	C	39	D				
40	D	40	B				
41	A	Correct:					
42	C						
Correct:							

SCORING SHEET : PRACTICE TEST 2

Test 2- Section 1 Reading		Test 2- Section 2 Writing and Language		Test 2- Section 3 Math No-Calculator		Test 2- Section 4 Math Calculator	
Q#	Answer	Q#	Answer	Q#	Answer	Q#	Answer
1	B	1	B	1	B	1	C
2	A	2	A	2	A	2	A
3	C	3	D	3	A	3	C
4	B	4	D	4	C	4	B
5	B	5	D	5	B	5	D
6	A	6	D	6	D	6	A
7	C	7	D	7	C	7	C
8	A	8	A	8	C	8	D
9	D	9	C	9	A	9	B
10	C	10	C	10	D	10	B
11	B	11	D	11	1.13	11	D
12	B	12	B	12	28	12	C
13	A	13	D	13	5/3	13	A
14	D	14	C	Correct:		14	B
15	C	15	A			15	B
16	C	16	C			16	C
17	B	17	D			17	B
18	D	18	D			18	B
19	D	19	C			19	C
20	A	20	D			20	D
21	A	21	A			21	A
22	B	22	B			22	9/4
23	D	23	B			23	5/4
24	C	24	C			24	1/4
25	C	25	A			25	584
26	B	26	B			Correct:	
27	A	27	D				
28	A	28	C				
29	C	29	B				
30	B	30	D				
31	C	31	A				
32	A	32	D				
33	A	33	B				
34	D	34	A				
35	D	35	D				
36	A	36	C				
37	B	37	B				
38	D	38	B				
39	B	39	D				
40	D	40	C				
41	A	Correct:					
42	B						
Correct:							

SCORING SHEET : PRACTICE TEST 3

Test 3- Section 1 Reading		Test 3- Section 2 Writing and Language		Test 3- Section 3 Math No-Calculator		Test 3- Section 4 Math Calculator	
Q#	Answer	Q#	Answer	Q#	Answer	Q#	Answer
1	B	1	D	1	D	1	B
2	C	2	D	2	C	2	A
3	B	3	B	3	C	3	B
4	A	4	D	4	A	4	D
5	D	5	A	5	C	5	C
6	B	6	C	6	B	6	D
7	A	7	C	7	B	7	A
8	C	8	B	8	B	8	C
9	D	9	B	9	C	9	C
10	B	10	C	10	C	10	B
11	D	11	B	11	0	11	C
12	C	12	C	12	7	12	A
13	A	13	D	13	2	13	D
14	B	14	D	Correct:		14	D
15	C	15	B			15	D
16	C	16	C			16	B
17	A	17	A			17	D
18	C	18	A			18	B
19	B	19	C			19	A
20	A	20	D			20	C
21	C	21	C			21	B
22	C	22	C			22	34.3
23	D	23	B			23	3
24	B	24	D			24	34
25	D	25	B			25	22
26	C	26	D			Correct:	
27	B	27	A				
28	C	28	D				
29	A	29	C				
30	C	30	D				
31	D	31	A				
32	C	32	D				
33	B	33	C				
34	A	34	C				
35	B	35	D				
36	D	36	B				
37	C	37	A				
38	A	38	B				
39	C	39	A				
40	A	40	C				
41	A	Correct:					
42	B						
Correct:							

Enter the number of correct answers from the three practice tests in the table below.

PSAT 8/9 * 3 PRACTICE TESTS * SCORE ANALYSIS							
Test	Reading	Writing	Reading+Writing Total	Math-No Calc	Math-Calc	Math Total	Test Total
Test-1							
Max	42	40	82	13	25	38	120
Read/Write Scaled:	/82*720=		Math Scaled:	/38*720=		Test-1 Scaled:	
Test-2							
Max	42	40	82	13	25	38	120
Read/Write Scaled:	/82*720=		Math Scaled:	/38*720=		Test-2 Scaled:	
Test-2							
Max	42	40	82	13	25	38	120
Read/Write Scaled:	/82*720=		Math Scaled:	/38*720=		Test-3 Scaled:	

Notes:

- Your raw scores will be scaled to a maximum of 720 in Reading & Writing and 720 in Math for a total test maximum of 1440.
- CollegeBoard does not publish the scaling formula. To get a rough estimate, use the following formula based on direct proportion:
  - Estimated Scaled Reading+Writing Score= (reading+writing total raw score/82) * 720
  - Estimated Math Score= (math total raw score/38) * 720
  - Estimated Total Score= Estimated Reading Score + Estimated Math Score
  - Round the scores to the nearest ten.
- From the table above, identify the sections where you are weak or strong.
- The following workbooks, available from Amazon, will help you to focus on specific areas of the tested topics. Search for "PSAT 8/9" in Amazon.
  - PSAT 8/9 Math Workbook
  - PSAT 8/9 Reading/Writing Workbook

Made in the USA
Lexington, KY
01 September 2018